A Theology for the Rest of Us

Arthur Yavelberg

For information, contact
MSI Press
1760-F Airline Highway, #203
Hollister, CA 95023

Cover designed by Carl Leaver
Cover Graphic by Peter Hermes Furian/ShutterStock

Copyeditor: Dr. Geri Henderson

Library of Congress Number: 2021900066

ISBN: 978-1-950328-86-4

Contents

A Theology for the Rest of Us

These are trying times, as they say. I am older now—way past the 40 years of age that was the boundary for baby boomers for any kind of trust. I personally remember the race riots of the 60's, the demonstrations against the Viet Nam War and the cynicism of political authority born of Watergate. I have studied enough history to be more than a little familiar with the Civil War, the Great Depression, and when the United States seriously considered the proposition that "What this country needs is a dictator!" Today's challenges seem to pale in comparison. Nevertheless, the big difference is that today's challenges are today's challenges. The past is important and can have lessons that can be helpful, but those lessons must be understood and applied today for them to be any good.

Maybe the most frustrating problem facing so many today is the feeling of helplessness that comes from feeling overwhelmed. Access to information, through the Internet and other media, was supposed to be a panacea, a way to access information so that we can all make intelligent choices for ourselves. As it happens however, there has been so much information, tsunamis of data from all kinds of experts on just about any topic imaginable, that most of us, the rest of us, are drowning and panicked.

It is in this context that I offer this little book, *A Theology for the Rest of Us*. "Theology" is a broad, intimidating term for a host of questions having to do with the meaning and source of life and all existence. Like any other topic, there are many experts with all kinds of degrees and weighty theses and analyses. Their language is often esoteric—complicated, they usually say, because the topic is complicated and the language must be precise. I suspect, however, that some of that complicated language is less about precision and more about preserving their authority and power. "I know these big words and you don't, so you need to listen to me because I'm smarter than you."

Let me say from the outset that I am not smarter than you. I don't have a lot of university degrees or acronyms after my name. I also don't have a long white beard or colorful robes or an exotic accent. I'm someone who has read a lot, travelled a little and, maybe most important of all, asked a lot of questions. I assure you: I have had no grand epiphany, no extraordinary experience where the heavens have opened and revealed the presence of The Almighty Who has resolved all my doubts and insecurities. I have simply looked at the world around me and its history and tried to make some sense of it all. I do not have all the answers, but I have come to enough of a direction to feel like I have a better idea as to where I am going and that keeps me from feeling lost, at least most of the time.

While this book is mine and makes sense to me, I doubt there is anything truly new here. Many of these ideas are quite old, in fact. I just may be presenting them in a more understandable way. This is not a peremptory defense for any inadvertent plagiarism. I taught middle school for many years and, if I had any strengths, it had to do with explaining ideas to adolescents with examples they could follow. I never felt like I was talking down to them

Rather, I felt like we were on a journey together trying to make sense of all the ways people have thought and behaved in the past. Sometimes we made more sense than others, but it was always intriguing and fun.

Note that this process involved "all the ways." Over the millennia of human history, there have been countless theologies, philosophies, metaphysics—with leaders and followers just as diverse. My guess is that people selected faiths or lack thereof as much as reflections of their personalities as because of any intrinsic logical persuasiveness. As a result, I have allowed myself the freedom to pick and choose what makes sense to me and what does not. While every system of thought may have something of value, not every system of thought has everything of value for everyone.

I do not say that lightly, by the way, and you should not underestimate the risks of such an approach. People are social animals by nature and religions (and, for these purposes, I include atheism as a religion in the sense that it is a system of faith) are social communities where there is considerable pressure to conform. That is not a blanket criticism or rejection of all religions. Peer pressure is not always a bad thing and finding a group of like-minded people can help encourage us to persist when the inevitable doubts and frustrations of life appear. How to balance one's unique ideas with the needs of a group for cohesion is no easy task. It is probably true that everyone has their crises of faith, but not everyone is prepared to acknowledge and address those crises openly and consciously. Such people are not going to take too kindly to those with questions they themselves have exerted great psychic energy to repress. Therefore, while just about everyone espouses the value of "independent, critical thinking," just about everyone expects that the results of that independent, critical thinking will validate their own. When those results do not coincide, it is seldom a pretty picture. To the degree you value these social attachments, be warned that such theological explorations may leave you alone on your journey.

If you have any doubts along those lines, consider the fates of those religious personalities who dared to challenge their contemporary religions. In the Biblical *Book of Genesis*, for example, Abraham begins Judaism—and, with it, Western monotheism— by abandoning his homeland, Ur, and everything he associated with civilization as he follows God's command to "Leave your native country, your relatives, and your father's family to a land that I will show you" (Gen. 12). Siddhartha, the Buddha-to-be, similarly left his family and his father's palace to seek enlightenment. Lao Tzu may have understood what was in store for him as well as he left his Chinese homeland, writing his *Tao Te Ching* at the request of a ferryman taking him to his disappearance. Muhammed had to flee for his life once he started telling his story, escaping the Mecca of his youth to Medina. And then, of course, there is the most dramatic example of all: Jesus is actually crucified for daring to defy the religious expectations of his time. So, should you develop any divine inspirations on your own that deviate from those around you whom you have come to know and love, do not expect to be greeted by adoring smiles and gratitude.

I should also caution you that there are many who believe that such speculations are, at best, a waste of time and, at worst, a dangerous distraction that diverts energies from confronting the real problems of suffering facing humanity. The Buddha himself proposed his "Allegory of the Poisoned Arrow." This is a tale of a man shot by a poisoned arrow. Before he will allow treatment, he insists on answering questions such as "Who shot the arrow?" "Why did this person shoot me?" "What is the composition of the arrow?" "What kind of poison was used?" "Where did it come from?" Given the time involved in trying to answer these questions, the victim eventually dies from his untreated wound. For the Buddha, then, it is far better and more productive to address the issue of human suffering than to engage in endless, fruitless metaphysical speculation.

However, the Buddha also taught "Be ye lamps unto yourselves." (Carus, trans. 1894, (93:13)) In other words, he said that only those beliefs that make sense to the individual should be followed—and that included his own teachings. Those of us who are "distracted" ("plagued" might be more accurate) by such metaphysical speculations know that ignoring them is not an option. Not everyone is a diabetic so not everyone needs insulin. However, those of us who are metaphysical diabetics do ourselves no favors by pretending otherwise. We may never reach absolute certainty, but we are reasonably confident that we can make enough progress to make a difference in living our day-to- day lives. It is in that spirit that I have written this book. Hopefully, it will provide some illumination that will help you find your own way in these dark times.

1

Teleology

"What's it all about, Alfie?" (Dione Warwick)

Imagine coming into a large, dark room. You flip on the lights and find there are many tables, 50 or more, that are set with centerpieces, dishes, glasses, silverware, napkins and tablecloths. In the front of the room, there is a row of chairs with a podium and a microphone in the middle of the room.

So? What goes through your mind?

If your answer is "Nothing" or "All these things got here by accident somehow...maybe random storage...," then you can stop reading now. That is not to say you are wrong. After all, you were not there when these items were placed in the room; nor did you meet the individual responsible for putting these items there. There is simply no way of knowing "for sure" whether all this stuff was placed in the room intentionally for some purpose. You also might not care one way or the other. Therefore, it would be understandable if you just turned out the lights and left the room to go about whatever business does concern you.

However, if you have any curiosity about such questions: "Why are these things here?" "Who put them here?" and "What are these things for?" then you are asking the kinds of questions that lead you to a book like this. Alas, I also was not present when these items were placed in the room and nor did I meet the person responsible for putting the items in the room. Therefore, I have no way of knowing "for sure" anything.

Having said that, and with all due respect to Sherlock Holmes, it seems to me a fair number of inferences can be made from the information that is available. These tables and chairs are set; in other words, there is no evidence they were simply thrown into a random empty room for convenient storage. As these tables and chairs are set, it is very reasonable to assume that someone intentionally and intelligently placed these tables and chairs where they are. Unless there is additional information, maybe some banners, place cards or pictures on the walls, we may not know what the purpose was, but we can assume that someone somewhere had some purpose. That purpose may even have been to be available in case someone else might need a room, but that, too, qualifies as a purpose.

If this reasoning makes sense to you, then you essentially have a basis of believing in a Divine Intelligence or DI at work in the universe. I will avoid the term *God* as that means so many things to so many people that it would often be more confusing than helpful. But whatever label is used, the point is that all of what makes the universe the universe—all the natural laws, human intelligence, evolution, the functioning of the eye, the scent of flowers...all of it—is infinitely more complex than a room, however large, filled with intricately arranged furniture. If a room cannot be elaborately furnished at random, then neither can the universe.

The technical term for this line of reasoning is the *teleological argument* and it has been around a very long time. Still, there clearly are those who reject it. Some of these people are highly intelligent and I respect their viewpoints. I just don't see how they can look at the same universe and think of terms like *random* or *accident*. This is not a question of "blind faith" or "mysticism." It seems to me that there is an order inherent in the universe that is self-evident—rationally self-evident to the point where other conclusions are rationally implausible. The Psalmist is absolutely right when he declares: "The heavens proclaim the glory of God. The heavens declare His handiwork." (Ps. 19:1)

Further, those who say that they "put their faith in science" must assume the very rationality of the universe I am proposing. The scientific method is, after all, a way of generating and testing hypotheses as to the nature of reality based on observed, reliable principles—the results of which have to be consistent if they are to be accepted as "science." That is how diseases are cured. That is how technology advances. That is how our understanding of how the universe increases. To dismiss the framework in which such processing takes place as "arbitrary" or "accidental" strikes me as arbitrary to say the least.

So, in this context, if you are with me so far, I have "set the table," as it were, and we can move on.

2

The Identity of the Divine

"A rose by any other name..." (Shakespeare)

As compelling as the teleological argument may be, it does not say much about DI itself. Even the pronoun *itself* is itself problematic. Traditional references to God in the West use the pronoun *He* while at the same time admitting that God must be beyond gender. *He* may be expedient but is misleading and problematic, especially for those who see pervasive linguistic insinuations to perpetuate patriarchal authority. Of course, *She* has the same issues, though some believe that the nature of Creation is more accurately described as feminine—as in "Mother Nature." *Itself* has the advantage of being gender-neutral but suggests that DI is inanimate, unconscious and, maybe more important, impassive and uncaring. With these questions in mind, I will use the pronoun *S/He* and the invented "DI-self" for self-reflecting purposes which, while cumbersome, may convey some of the mysterious difficulties inherent in trying to discuss the Divine Intelligence responsible for all of Creation. That DI can refer to Divine Intelligence as well as the prefix meaning *double* may appeal to those determined to come up with esoteric interpretations. There are myriad possibilities—and none may be more accurate than any other.

The Bible may understand some of these nuances as well. That may be the reason there are so many names for God: Adonai, El Shaddai, HaMaKom, etc. Jewish tradition indicates that these names may be used to illustrate different aspects of God, such as power or compassion. The most explicit context comes in *Exodus 3* when Moses, about to undertake his mission to redeem the Israelites from Egyptian slavery, asks God which name he should use in talking about God to the people. "I will be who I will be." (*Ex.* 3:13) is the response. Some use the translation "I am who I am." Either way, the point is that God has no definite nature and, therefore, cannot have an all-inclusive name. People being people, though, want and maybe need a much more specific reference. As a result, they took the first Hebrew letters of the response—"Yod-heh-vav-heh" and turned them into yet one more name for God: Yahweh, or the later anglicized Jehovah. That this new name completely overturns the intent of God's response does not seem to bother anyone, maybe because the process of naming the Un-nameable gives people a sense of control, much like, for example, Adam's earlier naming of the animals in the Garden of Eden in *Genesis.*

Lao Tzu, in the most sacred text of Taoism, *The Tao Te Ching,* takes a much more direct approach. "The Tao that can be told is not the eternal Tao. The Nameless is the beginning of heaven and earth; the mother of the 10 thousand things (all of reality) (Lao Tzu, *Tao The Ching* 1:1-2)." The Tao is responsible for all creation, somehow emanating the complementary male and female principles that then lead to all of Creation. This is symbolized by the popular Taoist black/white circle in which each has its spot in the center of the other. The Tao is un-nameable and unknowable in itself because it is the source of all of Creation and is beyond the scope of language that describes that Creation.

Hinduism apparently approaches the question from the opposite direction. Anyone who has visited a Hindu temple, particularly in southern India that was less affected by the Muslim influences in the north, cannot help but see the practically infinite number of gods and goddesses in myriad forms, human and otherwise. Nevertheless, underlying all those forms is "Brahman" which does not seem to differ too much from the amorphous, mysterious Tao or the Biblical "I Will Be Who I Will Be."

Even so, as ineffable as this God/Tao/Brahman/Source/DI may be, that does not necessarily mean that nothing at all can be known. In the Bible, Moses asks God, "Show me your glory" (Ex 33:18). God responds by saying that that is impossible; should any human see God in His essential glory, that human would be so overwhelmed that s/he would die. "For you cannot see my face and live." (Ex 33:20) However, God does protect Moses in the cleft of a rock as He says, "I will make all my goodness pass before you...where you will see My back, but My face may not be seen." (*Ex*. 33:19, 23) It is not at all clear just what it is that Moses sees, but the message appears to be that, while God cannot be perceived directly, God can be inferred through His behavior.

That brings us to the debate regarding a third possible quality of DI. In the context of DI's behavior, the Teleological Proof establishes that DI is rational and creative. Simply put, existence exists and makes sense. Even the most atheistic scientist would agree that existence exists and makes sense. The question now is whether DI is "conscious," aware of the existence S/He has created. Both the Old and New Testaments of the Bible and the Koran in Islam make it very clear that God/Allah is fully conscious as to what goes on in His Creation. In Hinduism it seems that Brahman is aware of Creation through the myriad gods and goddesses, much like a person is conscious of the world through his or her senses.

Taoist scholars, however, for the most part, seem to say that the Tao is beyond consciousness just as the Tao is beyond all dualities as it is the source of all dualities. I think that is true, but that is not the same thing as saying the Tao is unconscious. Since the Tao is the source of all dualities, it must somehow include all dualities. In the West, that kind of statement makes no sense. How can something be both conscious and unconscious? Hard and soft? Male and female?

That, in fact, is one of the most appealing aspects of Taoism. In Western logic, "A is A and B is B." In Eastern logic, as in the Taoist symbol, "A is A *because* of B and B is B *because* of A." In other words, in the West things exist independently of each other. In the East, everything depends on everything else for its existence. Looked at objectively—assuming objectively is possible—it seems to me the Eastern approach makes more sense. After all, we would not have an understanding of *hard* without an understanding of *soft*. In fact, *hard* and *soft* are relative terms. A piece of paper is harder than water, but paper is softer than a rock, and a diamond is harder than a rock. It all depends on the context. With Taoism, then, it is not that the Tao is conscious or unconscious but that the Tao is somehow both.

From a scientific perspective, the question is actually easier. If the universe is "everything" and people who are conscious are included in that "everything," then the universe has to be "conscious" to at least a certain extent. It is important to remember that, scientifically speaking, the universe produced people and human consciousness, so the universe has to have some capacity for consciousness in order to produce it. It is like the sun and sunlight: the sun gives off rays of light, but the sun and its sunlight are not separate entities as one emanates from the other.

Therefore, it seems to me that the DI's consciousness, in addition to DI's rationality and creativity, is an area where science, religions East and West, whether monotheistic or polytheistic, agree. DI is aware of DI's rational Creation.

3

Divine Concern

"Tell me you'll love me for a million years. Then you can tell me we tried." (The Casinos)

For most people, this may be the most important topic in this book. "There are no atheists in a foxhole." In other words, people often look to God and religion in times of crisis; in times when they recognize and acknowledge their own fragility and ultimate helplessness. As the Danish existentialist Soren Kierkegaard describes it, these are the times *Of Fear and Trembling* (1843). Yes, a crisis is not necessarily a bad thing. A crisis can be a wake-up call—the understanding, finally, that everything is not all right just as it is and that change, sometimes radical change, is necessary. But a crisis can also lead to terror, the terror of a past that is no longer viable and a future that is most uncertain, and terror can lead to paralysis and paralysis can lead to despair.

The benefits of theology in such times have not been historically all that clear. In fact, the Deism of the 17th and 18th Centuries, the Enlightenment, essentially proposed the god of the "banquet in waiting;" a dark, elegantly furnished ballroom, whereby there is a god who created the entire universe and all its intricate scientific laws and principles but afterward withdrew and now does not get involved in that universe or interact with people in any way. This god set the universe in motion, the "Prime Mover," and then went wherever gods go when their work is finished. This god makes sense in accounting for the rationality of the natural laws permeating the universe. This god makes no sense to a poor mother grieving over the loss of her child, a young man whose hopes have been dashed by some freakish, crippling accident, a once-thriving town that has been devastated by an earthquake, a....well, that list is endless. One who is tempted to quote a teleological argument as a comfort in such circumstances would be well advised to keep quiet.

The Taoism of China, which idealistic types laud as epitomizing all that is peace and harmony, fares no better and needs to be recognized for what it is. The Tao is the source of all dualities. The Taoist symbol includes BOTH the light and the dark in equal measure. Consequently, as hard as it is to imagine, the Tao incorporates both caring and apathy, compassion and anger, peace and war, etc. Evil is as much a part of the universe as the good. Since all dualities are interdependent, eliminating the evil means eliminating the good as well. In this context, the grieving mother of a lost child may find the Tao more confusing than consoling

It gets worse. If a brilliant but apathetic deity is of no consolation to those who are grieving, imagine the impact of, say, a Jonathan Edwards. An American Colonial Protestant pastor, his depiction of the divine makes the Deist or Taoist look positively soothing,

The God that holds you over the pit of hell, much as one holds a spider, or some loathsome insect, over the fire, abhors you, and is dreadfully provoked. His wrath towards you burns like fire; he looks upon you as worthy of nothing else. (Edwards, 1741, p. 15)

As horrific as such imagery may be, it appears there is something of the human psyche that responds to such "fire and brimstone" throughout the ages. Maybe whatever misfortune one is confronting becomes more manageable if one believes it is the deserved result of sin. Nevertheless, it is difficult to move forward in hope when one is inevitably doomed to fail because of one's sinful nature.

The ancient Persian Zoroastrians avoid problems of divine apathy and/or fury by asserting there are two, eternally competing forces at work in the universe. Throughout the eons of time, the pristine Ahura Mazda marshals all the angelic powers of good versus the demonic minions of the repulsive Angra Mainyu. At the end of days, however, there will be a savior, the Saoshyant—yes, born of a virgin—who will defeat the forces of evil and everyone will be purified. Even so, it seems highly unlikely that a grieving mother of a lost child will find much comfort in the notion she must simply be patient for all eternity.

Western monotheistic religions have the same dilemma. If God created the universe, God has to be responsible for everything in the universe. Indeed, God Himself proclaims: "I form the light and create darkness. I make peace and create evil. I, the Lord, do all these things." (Is 45:7) In Islam, too, there is the controversy as to whether Allah creates both good and evil or that Allah just creates the good, whereas the evil comes from man (Asar, 2019). As more than one skeptic has observed: "If God is good and all-powerful, why is there evil? If God cannot prevent evil, He is not all-powerful. If God can prevent evil but does not, He is not good." Therefore, the case against DI's caring is a strong one. The proposition that DI does care seems salvageable only by compromising DI's power.

But maybe the situation is not so, well, black and white. The meaning of terms like *good* and *evil* seem simple enough, but simplicity is often misleading. Again, the Taoist symbol is black and white, but the two are not distinct halves. Rather, they are equal, but in a flowing motion, with the center of each in the midst of the other.

After all, what exactly do we mean by the term *evil*? It seems obvious that the term refers to "bad stuff," but *bad*—like all dualities—is a relative term. It assumes the follow-up question "bad for whom or what?" For example, I have seen any number of Disney-type stories or fables where some animal is "good, sweet, and innocent" and some other animal is "evil, mean, and criminal." Take the well-known story of the "Three Little Pigs." Here these good, sweet, innocent pigs are defending themselves against a wolf who wants to eat them, a wolf who is prepared to "huff and puff and blow your house down" to do so. The last pig saves the three of them by having built a sturdy home of brick that withstands all the wolf's huffing and puffing. Having outwitted the wolf, the pigs celebrate and the dejected wolf goes away. The stories generally end at this point, and the reader invariably smiles contentedly with the thought that justice has prevailed and the evil has been defeated.

That makes sense insofar as the pigs are concerned, but what about the wolf? The wolf goes away hungry and, assuming the wolf has his own family, it will go hungry as well. Is that "good?" If the wolf's wife was telling the tale, she would likely lament the state of a universe where pigs are devilishly clever and, as a result, where she and her children need to starve.

The truth is that "good" and "evil" depend on the perspective of an individual. If one can attain the much broader perspective of the Tao—perceiving the predicaments of the pigs *and* the wolf, then one can develop compassion for both. Ultimately all life survives by consuming itself, though it may appear as if "this" is eating "that." "This" and "that" are all "life."

Of course, again, such an insight may not be of any comfort to that grieving mother who lost a son. However, helping that mother develop something of that broader perspective just might be. While the Buddha contributed little to the metaphysical discussion regarding teleology, it is here in the case of broadening one's perspective that the Buddha can be especially helpful.

The story is told of a woman who is agonizing with grief over the loss of her son. She approaches the Buddha desperate for his help. Simply put, she wants the Buddha to bring her son back to life. The Buddha considers her request and, after some thought, he says softly, "I can bring your son back to life. For me to do so, you must go through the village and bring me a mustard seed from a family who has not suffered such a loss. Bring me that mustard seed and I will do as you ask" (Bjordal, 2020). The poor mother is thrilled and immediately starts going house to house, door to door, in search of that mustard seed. In so doing, she tells her tale to every household. But while everyone is sympathetic, it turns out that every household has had its own share of terrible losses. It takes a while, but the mother comes to realize such losses are common to everyone; that they are a part of life itself. She returns to the Buddha and thanks him—not because he has brought her son back to life, but because he has made her realize that she is not alone.

The fact that life in the universe depends on life eating life does not necessarily mean that DI doesn't care. It simply means that seeing life as it is can help those who are grieving and sharing that experience in ways that only those who suffer can be essential to addressing that grief.

4

Alternatives to What Is

"Variety is the spice of life." (William Cowper)

Maybe another way to address the question, "Does DI care?" is to ask about possible alternatives to Creation. It is true that the universe has both good and evil, life and death, and creation and destruction. Couldn't it be otherwise? Theologically speaking, what about the Garden of Eden in the *Book of Genesis*? There everything was perfect, idyllic—until Adam and Eve ate of the fruit of the Tree of Knowledge. Even assuming they sinned and deserved some kind of punishment, at least to teach them a lesson that they should "Go and sin no more," why did they have to be banned from Paradise forever? Would it have been so terrible had Adam and Eve eaten of the fruit of The Tree of Life as well and, in fact, lived as gods? And the LORD God said, "The man has now become like one of us, knowing good and evil. He must not be allowed to reach out his hand and take also from the tree of life and eat and live forever" (Gen. 3: 21-22). For many, God comes across as fearful, even petty, in this account.

But suppose, for argument's sake, God did allow Adam and Eve to live their immortal lives in the Garden of Eden. Would that be the necessary proof that God/DI cares? Alan Watts, the writer/speaker/philosopher (I would say *guru*, but I believe he would have found the term offensive and contrary to his teachings.) who popularized the Eastern religious approach in the West during the turbulent 1960's, would disagree.

Imagine having everything you could possibly want. Everything...for all time. That would be great, for sure, but for how long? After years and decades and centuries and millennia of having everything you ever wanted and having everything turn out just the way you wanted it to be, you would inevitably get bored. For example, what gives fiction of any genre its ability to entertain is its potential for surprise. There have to be real challenges to overcome: the possibility of defeat, the chance to lose. Even Superman had to have his Kryptonite to be taken seriously. Otherwise, his victories are just too easy. Similarly, the thrill of gambling is due to the real chance one may lose. The excitement of skydiving comes from the threat of death. Whatever the activity, the pleasure is not so pleasant if everything is consistently, predictably pleasant. Therefore, would eternal life in a perfect Garden of Eden where everything turned out fine all the time really demonstrate that God/DI cared? Or would such a fate be life in a gilded cage where the very joys of life become twisted into an eternal torment of boredom?

Pierre Teilhard de Chardin, an early 20th Century Catholic priest who was a renowned paleontologist and had seen the horrors of World War I firsthand in the French ambulance corps, had a somewhat different take. Flowers are beautiful. Which would be preferable: artificial flowers that would stay as brightly colorful and appear as fresh indefinitely? Or would real flowers, brightly colorful and truly fresh, be preferable, even though, as real flowers, they would inevitably wither, decay and die? For de Chardin, ultimately it is death itself that allows us to cherish what life has to offer. Permanence, however beautiful, is not a blessing, but a curse.

That impermanence is the essence of the Buddha's teachings regarding how to end human suffering. For the Buddha, suffering is caused by human attachment, specifically, the desire that that which is impermanent be permanent. His "Eight-Fold Path" is essentially a method for recognizing impermanence and eliminating the attachment to the desire for permanence in order to end suffering. We may want everything we want and enjoy to last forever. Even so, it is not only that that is impossible. Properly understood, it is not even desirable.

While it is understandable to want pleasure and avoid pain, the universe does not and cannot provide consistent pleasure and no pain. Nor would we want it to even if we could have the universe work that way. Does that demonstrate the DI really does not care about people because if DI did care, the universe would be able to work that way—to provide consistent pleasure and no pain? Doesn't the fact that DI could not and did not create a universe with perpetual pleasure and no pain mean that DI really is not all-powerful?

I don't think so. Logically, it does not follow that, say, because DI cannot add 2 + 2 and get 3 or 47 or 913, it means that DI is not all-powerful. It simply means that to be all-powerful, DI can only do whatever is possible. That is not a limitation. That is reality.

5

Free Will

"Ecstasy ain't free." (Melissa Etheridge)

No discussion of teleology—that the scientific laws of the universe demonstrate there must have been intent and purpose in the Creation of the universe—or divine caring can be complete without including the topic of free will. As with teleology, I know there are very intelligent, respected experts of many kinds who reject the existence of free will. There is actually a long-standing history of determinism. Ancient Greeks like Democritus believed, like many modern scientists, that if all the variables involved with the motion of atoms could be measured, any and all actions including human behavior would be predictable. The process would be similar to a game of billiards. If one could measure the force and direction of the cue ball, the resistance of the felt table covering, the weight of the other billiards, one should be able to calculate the final resting place of each billiard ball. According to this rationale, it does not matter if the tools exist that can precisely conduct these measurements. The point is that they are measurable in principle and the results are predetermined, even if unknown.

There are modern neurologists who come to the same basic conclusion. They claim our ability to choose is an illusion and point to studies that indicate the relevant part of the brain is active before a decision is conscious, indicating the choice was actually the result of the brain's neural interactions and not some conscious selection. These studies are preliminary and involve rather simple behaviors—whether or not to pick up a pencil, for example—and not everyone agrees that they establish a deterministic view of the universe. Still, there are certainly many scientists who lean in that direction.

Although I recognize that my understanding of the mathematics and science involved is very limited, it nevertheless seems to me that, like teleology, the existence of free will is self-evident. That is not just a matter of conscious impression. The very question, "Is there free will?" and the argument "There is no free will" themselves assume the existence of free will. After all, what is the point of raising a question or trying to persuade a listener if both the question and the answers are predetermined? Just about all human behavior and interactions, the overwhelming majority of which are far more complicated than whether or not to pick up a pencil, presume the human ability to make choices. That ability is not unlimited and is impacted by both internal and external factors. Different individuals with different talents, ages, intelligence, etc. have more or fewer options available to them than others. The same is true of where one is born, to which family, in what time period, and the like. But even with limitations, the essence of the ability to make choices remains, even if that ability is relative.

The development of Quantum Physics seems to add some intriguing possibilities in this discussion. According to Newtonian Physics, with all of Isaac Newton's Laws or Motion, calculus, and the like, the deterministic "billiards game" formulation was hard to avoid. Given the right instruments and a knowledge of all the relevant variables, one could in principle predict exactly what would happen once the cue ball was struck.

At the subatomic level of Quantum Physics, however, that does not appear to be the case. While freely (?!) admitting my limited understanding of the topic, a perplexed status I apparently share with a great many others, including the illustrious Albert Einstein ((who insisted he could not believe in a God who plays dice with the universe) (Einstein, 1946p. 146)) according to the Heisenberg Uncertainty Principle of Quantum Physics, such measurements and the consequent predictability are in principle impossible. At the subatomic level, there are only probabilities. Minute portions of light, quanta, for instance, behave as either a particle or a wave, depending on whether their location or speed is being measured. Worse yet, the very act of attempting the measurements seem to affect that which is being measured in such a way that the results are altered. Therefore, since the notion of determinism depends on the mathematical application of physical laws, it turns out that the mathematics of those physical laws in Quantum Physics yields only probabilities, not deterministic results. While Quantum Physics is still in its relatively early stages of development and is controversial, though less and less controversial as time passes, the point in this context is that science no longer has the sort of absolute power to veto belief in free will.

If that is the case regarding free will and science, what does it mean for theology? It is interesting that the issue of divine omniscience and free will historically seems to be more of an issue in the West than in the East. In the East, free will is assumed. For example, in the Hindu scripture, *The Bhagavad Gita*, the warrior Arjuna faces choice after choice after choice. He has had the good sense to have selected the god Krishna as his charioteer, even though Krishna will not fight in any battle. There are times when Arjuna, however heroic he has been, begins to despair of all the carnage and its ultimate meaning. Krishna counsels Arjuna that, as a warrior, he needs to fight because it is in his nature as a warrior to fight, irrespective of the results. In this context, it seems clear that Krishna does not know what Arjuna will choose to do—whether to fight or not—but that lack of foreknowledge does not seem to trouble Krishna or whoever may have been the author of the text.

It is not clear where this question of God's omniscience and free will arose in the West. The supposed conflict is not in the *Bible*. The Garden of Eden in the *Book of Genesis* is only the first example where people have choices to make, and God waits expectantly to see just what that choice will be. If anything, the entire Biblical theme of reward and punishment is based on the assumption that people have free will and that, up to Judgment Day at the End of Days, God Himself cannot know what any individual's fate may be. The same is true in Islam. After all, what would be the point of the command of prayer, formalized at five times a day, if Muslims did not have the spiritual freedom to disobey? For that matter, the term *Islam* itself means *surrender*. *Surrender* is a meaningful term only if there is an option not to surrender.

Even so, in the West, there seems to be a philosophical insistence that God must know everything and "everything" includes what people will do before they do it. Perhaps that is due to a number of verses like: "Nothing in all creation is hidden from God's sight. Everything is uncovered and laid bare before the eyes of him to whom we must give account" (Hebrews 4:13) There is also the philosophical tradition that essentially goes back to the classical Greek philosophers like Aristotle. Medieval theologians like the Christian St. Thomas Aquinas, the Jewish Maimonides, or the Muslim Averroes essentially adapted the idea of the "Unmoved Mover" as follows:

God is perfect.

That which is perfect does not change.

Since God is perfect, He cannot change.

God knows everything.

If God did not know everything, including people's choices with free will, God would come to learn something new once those choices were made.

If God learned something new, His knowledge would change.

If God's knowledge changed, God has changed.

If God had the capacity to change, God could not be perfect as that which is perfect does not change.

Religious theologians resolved this dilemma of God's omniscience and human free will by arguing that God's knowledge is different than human knowledge. God can see the span of human history all at once—say, like a filmmaker looking at an entire roll of film simultaneously. That reasoning was supposed to reconcile God's omniscience and human free will.

I, for one, am not convinced. If God can see the span of human history all at once, that means that in some sense all of human history is, well, history, i.e. everything has already happened. There is something odd in a *Back to the Future* sort of way about arguing that, at the beginning of time, God could see what human beings freely chose in the future, a future that is also in the past from God's perspective.

Besides, if the definition of *perfection* includes *non-changing,* I don't see *perfection* as *perfect* at all. If change and development are part of reality, to be unchanging is far less than perfect.

For me, the question is similar to the one having to do with whether the existence of evil compromises DI's omnipotence. In that context, it was not logical to conclude that God's omnipotence did not include the ability to add 2 + 2 and get 3 or some other number. Similarly, DI could not create a world with life, beauty, and peace without death, ugliness and war, all the dualities being dependent on one another. DI is omnipotent in the sense that DI can do anything that is possibly doable. In the question of free will then, DI is omniscient in the sense that DI can know anything that is possibly knowable.

I don't see how that compromises DI's omniscience in any meaningful sense of the word. For example, I like to play chess. With a rating of approximately 1700, I am a pretty mediocre player, not a beginner but not a "master" by any means. The present World Champion, Magnus Carlsen, has an approximate rating in the 2800 range. If we were to sit down and play a game of chess, it is fair to say that Carlsen would win. It is probably even fair to say it is a foregone conclusion that Carlsen would win. However, Carlsen cannot know exactly what moves I will make before I make them. Only when I make my moves can Carlsen know what moves I have made and then make his counter moves that will guide the game to his victory. In this scenario, the fact that Carlsen does not know what moves I will make does not mean his ability is limited. It just means that even Magnus Carlsen, the best chess grandmaster in the world, can only know what is knowable. He will win, but he will win by following the rules of the game. In the realm of theology, DI, has created the rules of the game. One of these rules is, and has to be, free will. DI, therefore, implicitly agrees to play by the rules. As Abraham challenges God in anticipation of the destruction of Sodom and Gomorrah, “Will not the Judge of the earth act justly?” (Gen. 18:25)

6

Implications of Free Will

"Freedom's just another word for nothin' left to lose."
(Janis Joplin)

So, maybe free will is part of the fabric of the universe. In fact, maybe it is one of those dualities that complements all the others: free/determined makes it possible for there to be happy/sad, love/hate, war/peace, and the like. There are even those who would go so far as to say that free will is the key for humans to be able to appreciate the extraordinary beauty and wonders of all Creation...or not. But clearly free will does not always mean that choices are good. Inevitably, if people have the capacity to make good choices, they must also have the capacity to make bad choices. People can be compassionate and mean, caring and sadistic.

One of the sharpest arguments against the desirability of freedom comes from the early 19th Century Russian novelist, Fyodor Dostoyevsky. In *The Brothers Karamazov,* the atheist Ivan challenges his priestly, perhaps naive, brother Alexey with "Imagine that you are creating a fabric of human destiny with the object of making men happy in the end... but that it was essential and inevitable to torture to death only one tiny creature ... And to found that edifice on its unavenged tears: would you consent to be the architect on those conditions? Tell me, and tell me the truth!" (1880, p. 308).

The argument is straightforward: if the price of reality and the potential for human happiness requires the tragic, unjustified suffering of one being—not necessarily a human being—then that reality and human happiness are not worth it.

It is not hard to find examples of bad choices. All of human history and literature is filled with all kinds of horrendous tales of senseless savagery. To pick just one graphic illustration comes from another novel by Dostoyevsky, *Crime and Punishment.* Here Raskolnikov is having a dream. There is a peasant, Mikolta, with a cart who wants to transport a group of drunken men. The cart is pulled by an old mare which is in no way able to carry such a load. The peasant is furious and starts beating the "wretched nag." A crowd gathers, with some yelling that the peasant is no Christian and others laughing, shouting encouragement, and making suggestions as to just how to beat the defenseless horse. "In the eyes! In the eyes!!" The crowd starts singing with the entertainment as every moment finds the peasant more and more enraged,-proclaiming that "It's my goods! I'll do as I choose!!" (1886, p. 58) seemingly to justify flailing at the horse over and over again. The ragged mare pulls and tugs but cannot budge its load. Finally, mercifully, the exhausted horse just dies.

Rashkolnikov cannot believe what he has seen. In the dream "the poor boy, beside himself, made his way screaming, through the crowd to the sorrel nag, put his arms round her bleeding dead head and kissed it, kissed the eyes and kissed the lips. Then he jumped up and flew in a frenzy with his little fists out at Mikolka. At that instant, his father, who had been running after him, snatched him up and carried him out of the crowd. 'Come along, come! Let us go home,' he said to him. 'Father! Why did they ... kill ... the poor horse!' he sobbed, but his voice broke and the words came in shrieks from his panting chest. 'They are drunk. They are brutal; it's not our business!' said his father. He put his arms round his father, but he felt choked, choked. He tried to draw a breath, to cry out—and woke up" (1886, p. 59).

Such horrific tales are not at all rare. They take place every single day somewhere around the world and, with the Internet and the "information highway," no one can even plead ignorance and glibly prattle on about how "This is the best of all possible worlds." Who is then prepared to self-righteously cast the first stone at Ivan Karamazov or even say to him "Go and blaspheme no more."

But it gets even worse. Peasants and most people can be defended, if not fully exonerated, by their ignorance. They themselves have invariably been brutalized in their own ways and, as a result, have their own rage and fears that they vent on others. In the context of teleology and religion, however, one would expect the learned and loving religious leaders to help people understand how to use their freedom wisely and compassionately.

Not so, contends Ivan Karamazov. In "The Grand Inquisitor," he tells the tale of how Jesus actually did come back to earth in medieval Spain during the Spanish Inquisition. When the unaware guards bring him to the Grand Inquisitor, instead of gratefully welcoming him whom humanity has desperately needed and longed for throughout history, the Grand Inquisitor has Jesus thrown in the dungeon. There he confronts the supposed Messiah, arguing that he and his message of spiritual freedom is a dangerous threat to the vast majority of people who have no realistic ability to handle such freedom. It may be that "man does not live by bread alone," but most are more obsessed with their bellies than with their souls. "Feed men, and then ask of them virtue! That's what they'll write on the banner they'll raise against Thee and with which they will destroy Thy temple" (1886, p. 278).

That is why the Church, and the Church alone, because the Church alone understands the nature of humanity and reality, must control people and make sure to prevent the inevitable evil that would be the outcome if people realized and used their free will. "Freedom, free thought and science, will lead them into such straits and will bring them face to face with such marvels and insoluble mysteries, that some of them, the fierce and rebellious, will destroy themselves," the Inquisitor says. "Others, rebellious but weak, will destroy one another while the rest, weak and unhappy, will crawl fawning to our feet" (1886, p. 325).

Therefore, according to the Grand Inquisitor, the Church has a moral obligation to control people, deprive them of their freedom, but feed them so they are blissful in their ignorance. In fact, it is the Devil who offers people what they truly need while Jesus's teachings of spiritual freedom lead to nothing but death and destruction.

Dostoyevsky paints a bleak picture indeed. Free will may be real, but it is not worth the price of suffering. The Church recognizes this and must act to eliminate free will as much as possible. In this context, it would be easy to expect that Ivan Karamazov is Dostoyevsky's mouthpiece for a world view that free will leads only to evil and disastrous tragedy.

That conclusion is not so certain, however. Father Zossima, a saint of a monk who was Alexey's teacher, recognizes the enormous potential for evil. In fact, he recognizes that monks, far from being better than anyone else, could actually at heart be the worst of humanity—which is why they need to sequester themselves in abbeys and seminaries away from the world. Having said that, Father Zossima on his death bed voices what may be Dostoyevsky's only possible answer to the dilemmas posed by free will:

Love one another, Fathers,' said Father Zossima, as far as Alyosha could remember afterward. 'Love God's people because (the monk) is responsible to all men for all and everything, for all human sins, national and individual, only then the aim of our seclusion is attained. This knowledge is the crown of life for the monk and for every man. For monks are not a special sort of men, but only what all men ought to be. Only through that knowledge, our heart grows soft with infinite, universal, inexhaustible love. Then every one of you will have the power to win over the whole world by love and to wash away the sins of the world with your tears.... (1886, p. 202)

It may be that Ivan is right insofar as the potential of free will for evil is concerned and the terrible, terrible suffering it can cause. The Grand Inquisitor may also be right that most people cannot handle free will and that it may be best for all concerned if religious authorities filled their bellies and emptied their souls. But it is also possible that Father Zossima is right that love has the power to redeem the worse that evil has to offer. After all, the Taoist maintains that all dualities balance each other out and Isaac Newton himself maintained that "For every action there is an equal and opposite reaction."

In any event, for good or ill, the debate about free will validates what Sarah Connor famously said in the science fiction *The Terminator* movies, "The future is not set. There is no fate other than what we make for ourselves" (Cameron, 1984).

7

Who to Believe

"You're not the boss of me!" (just about any 7th grader)

Assuming the existence of free will, given the stakes involved—both for the individual and, in today's highly technological, interconnected world, for all humanity—it is obviously imperative that people use their freedom to choose wisely. Dostoyevsky's "Grand Inquisitor" and Father Zossima are both right. Thousands of years of terrible suffering, death and destruction are more than ample testimony as to just what happens when people make the wrong decisions.

But how can one make sure to choose wisely? Access to information is supposed to be essential to choosing wisely and there is certainly ample information on any topic imaginable today. Unfortunately, there is so much information available today that it has practically become more of an obstacle than an aid. As I understand it, a typical Sunday edition of *The New York Times* has more information in it than the entire body of knowledge available in the Renaissance. Far more intimidating is the Internet where there is an infinite amount of information available on an infinite number of topics. How can one ever be able to sift through all that data to come to good decisions about anything?

Yes, one can consult with experts. However, the reason why any decision is difficult is because there are invariably different expert opinions. When it comes to medicine, for example, I have never understood the popular advice to "Always get a second opinion." Suppose one does get a second opinion? On what basis does one choose one opinion over the other? Every reasonable expert will have comparable credentials and will present their recommendations with compelling arguments. To prefer one over the other presumes superior understanding than either of them—in which case, why bother going to experts to begin with?

Combine too much information with too many experts and the result is ever-increasing specialization. The joke is that experts have become so specialized that they know more and more about less and less—to the point where they know absolutely everything about absolutely nothing! The problem with the joke is that, when someone needs to make an important decision that can affect many lives, it just isn't very funny.

This dilemma is no different in theology and religion. If it is next to impossible to make informed choices about day-to-day life where there is a great deal of information, how can one trust one's judgment regarding metaphysical questions, *metaphysics* literally meaning *above physics*? Again, there is a lot of information and a lot of experts, but one needs to have a way of differentiating between it all.

Religious authorities, particularly in Western, monotheistic religions, often have a simple answer to such questions: you don't, so you can't. In other words, like the Grand Inquisitor, the assumption is that people don't have any way to sift through all the available data by themselves, they don't have any way to differentiate between all the available experts, and the stakes are way too high to allow for mistakes. Therefore, the religious authorities need to make those decisions for their followers. To reject those authorities is to add the sin of hubris to one's ignorance. As a result, those individuals who insist on making decisions for themselves must be punished and must not be allowed to contaminate the rest of the group.

Unfortunately, the historical record with Western religions is pretty consistent in this regard. Words like *heresy, blasphemy,* and *excommunication* are much more common in Judaism, Christianity and Islam than in Taoism, Buddhism, and Hinduism. The same is true of the term *orthodox.* Etymologically Greek in origin *orthos* meaning *correct* and *doxa* meaning *belief*' the notion that there is one and only "correct belief" is manifest in the very first of the Biblical Ten Commandments, "Thou shall have no other gods before me." The reason seems obvious: Taoism and Buddhism do not focus on gods and, in Hinduism, there are so many different gods that particular beliefs do not seem to matter. As with any organized community, there are common ideas, rituals and practices that keep religious groups together, but the notion of insisting on dogma is not nearly as present in the East as in the West.

As a result, leaders in Western religions, whether out of genuine concern for the welfare of their followers or to protect their own power, reserve to themselves the authority to interpret God's will. These figures do not even allow God to intervene. In Judaism, the Rabbis of the Talmudic Period, roughly from 70 to 700 CE, declared that there was no more prophecy and canonized what to include in the Old Testament and what to exclude as Apocrypha. The Councils of Carthage and Hippo did the same with the New

Testament around the year 400 CE, rejecting any material like the Gnostic Gospels as inauthentic. Islam recognizes that Allah has had six prophets—Adam, Noah, Abraham, Moses, Jesus, and Muhammed—but Muhammed is the last and the greatest prophet. Followers of earlier prophets are respected as "People of the Book, "well, respected more or less, depending on the time period and geographical location, but followers of declared prophets like the Baha'i who came later were denounced and persecuted.

This monotheistic mindset has led to all kinds of wars between and within these religions. Orthodox Jewish sects excommunicate each other, Protestants battle Catholics, Shia Muslims constantly war with Sunni Muslims, and each of these has subsets far too numerous to list. Historically, when monotheistic religions have political power, there have been instances of forced conversions and persecutions—again, too many to list. That is not to say there have not been religious wars in the East. To this day one can visit temples where Hindu and Buddhist images have been defaced and replaced depending on which religion was in power at any particular time, but these seem less pronounced in the East and, more important, this intolerance is not consistent with their religious theologies.

In any event, in the context of *A Theology for the Rest of Us*, DI has created a universe in which people have free will. The ordered teleology of the universe makes it more plausible that there is only one "DI." The joke that "A camel is a horse made by committee" makes a lot of sense. In fact, all these religions East and West seem to agree there is one Source for all that exists, although there are significant disagreements as to whether there are intermediaries between that one Source and humanity. Problems, often with disastrous consequences, arise not only when one claims to know exactly what that Source is or who the intermediaries may be, but also when one feels compelled to force that certitude on others, whether within or outside the group. If DI has created the universe as a format in which people can have free will, to deprive people of free will is the most primary of sins. Further, to claim that one needs to deprive people of their free will out of love for them—otherwise, they and humanity will face the most dire of consequences—is a claim borne of pretense, self-interest, or delusion. How can presuming to know what the Lord of all Creation wants for each and every individual in each and every time period and location be anything other than the most extreme form of hubris?

Therefore, people have a divine obligation to think for themselves. However, that does not mean that people have to be totally alone as they process how to make those decisions. There are and have been many teachers. They go by different names and appear differently in different locations so that the message can be understood. In Hinduism, for example, Krishna can take any form imaginable in order to be able to relate to the individual as needed. But it is also true that deceivers go by different names and appear differently in different locations. How can one distinguish between a truly divine messenger and a false prophet?

As indicated above, the first clue is whether the individual takes the position that "You must follow my teachings or else!" The claim to a monopoly when it comes to spiritual wisdom is perhaps the most important indicator to look elsewhere. On the other hand, if someone offers teachings as teachings, allowing the student to decide what to accept and what to reject, then there may be something of value there. The Buddha's dictum that we should believe nothing, no matter where we read it, or who said it, no matter if he himself said it, unless it agrees with our own reason and our own common sense (Thera, 1994)) is probably the best standard in this regard. Similarly, not only do Buddhists not believe that the Buddha had a monopoly on spiritual wisdom. They also believe that everyone has the potential to become a "Buddha" in the sense of becoming "awakened." That does not happen by blindly following anyone, including the Buddha. That happens through genuine introspection and meditation, a process unique to each individual as each individual is different.

By the way, whether Jesus falls into this category is controversial. His statement that "I am the way, the truth and the life. None may approach my Father except through me" (John 14:6) suggests that Jesus believed he had just such a monopoly— and those who make a point of quoting this passage claim that same monopoly, albeit in His name. Historically the Catholic Church has taken the same position. For example, there is the pronouncement of St Fulgentius around the year 500, "Not only all pagans, but also all Jews and all heretics and schismatics, who finish their lives outside the Catholic Church, will go into eternal fire..." (Most). There are many other similar declarations.

However, the Gnostic Gospels, texts about Jesus's teachings that were rejected by the Church, project a more universalistic tone. For example, in The Gospel of Thomas, Jesus is reported to have said: "The kingdom is inside of you and outside of you. When you come to know who you are, then you will know that you are the children of the living God" (Gospel of Thomas, Saying 3). In this context, Jesus comes across as a teacher who is trying to help everyone realize their own divine nature. Everyone is thus a "Son of God," if they can just see it.

The position of the Catholic Church has evolved as well. While still believing that Salvation is only possible through Jesus, it is possible that those who lived before Jesus, never heard of Jesus or follow other religious paths may still follow Jesus's path, if unwittingly. Surprisingly, the Second Vatican Council in 1962 began formalizing this understanding. The Council maintained that "all men form but one community" (Mirus, 2010). This is true as they "all stem from the one stock which God created to people the entire earth" and they "all share a common destiny, namely God," whose "providence, evident goodness, and saving designs extend to all men" (Mirus, 2010)

The issue is also controversial in Islam. There are verses in the Koran that reject the notion that Jews and/or Christians have any special standing relative to heaven. "The Jews and the Christians say, 'We are Allah's children and His beloved ones.' *Say*, 'Then why does He punish you for your sins?' No, you are humans from among His creatures. He forgives whomever He wishes and punishes whomever He wishes" (*Koran* 5:18). But there are also numerous sources like "But those who are faithless and deny Our signs, they shall be the inmates of the Fire and they shall remain in it forever" (*Koran* 2:39).

In any event, a good spiritual guide not only accepts there is no monopoly of spiritual wisdom. Such a teacher also recognizes that, since people are so different, the truth is that everyone must follow a different path. In addition, this kind of teacher is confident that DI cares about everyone and has the ability to help everyone reach that mountaintop. If the individual chooses not to follow this particular teacher, there will be others.

In this context, the question of personal morality often arises. Does a potential teacher have to be moral in order to be considered? While this is a popular standard, the historical record is not so clear. First, no one is perfect, so to demand moral purity from any potential guide is to dismiss guides altogether. Second, there have been any number of super-creative geniuses who were not at all moral in their own lives. Albert Einstein, Pablo Picasso, Nikola Tesla—none of these and many, many more were not paradigms of virtue, but they nevertheless had much to offer in their areas of expertise. That Einstein was an adulterer does not negate the value of his Theory of Relativity.

Having said that, spiritual teachers may be different. They, too, are human beings and, as such, cannot be expected to be perfect. In this case, there should be some degree of consistency between what they teach and what they practice. An easy target in this regard is the Christian pastor who extols the virtues of Jesus's teachings and yet lives in a palace and preaches in an enormous temple that outshines the Biblical Temple in Jerusalem. However, even this example is not so easy. If this pastor preaches the value of poverty, often to increase his own wealth, then, yes, this is the kind of hypocrisy that invalidates a potential spiritual guide. On the other hand, if this pastor preaches that material wealth is a sign of divine blessing, the so-called "Gospel of Wealth," then there is no inherent hypocrisy at all.

Alan Watts is another example. A brilliant writer and philosopher who introduced many in the West to the teachings of the East, he was also an alcoholic who eventually died of his drinking at 58. To characterize his behavior as an addiction may be objectively accurate, but he would argue that that term subtly undermines his life's work. For Watts, this life is to be enjoyed. "The problem is that people take too seriously what the gods intended for play" (Hunt, 2020). To hear Watts tell the story, he drank because he wanted to drink. To live a life without this pleasure would mean not truly living at all. One can judge Watts' behavior as one sees fit, but there was no inherent hypocrisy there (Steve, 2007).

Ultimately, the sign of a potential spiritual guide is that something about that guide resonates. It may not be possible to define, but "something" strikes a chord within us that just feels right and empowering. Of course, that is easy to say and many have been fooled by charlatans who know how to manipulate their delusions and fears. Even so, that is ok. If one selects a spiritual guide and that person turns out to be a false prophet, hopefully one learns from that experience and moves on. Again, no one is perfect and if we had perfect judgment, we would not need a spiritual guide to begin with. Patience is also a virtue. And if the Creator of all the Universe truly cares about us, DI will make sure that we will learn whatever we need to learn in order to get where we need to go, however long it takes.

Martin Buber, a Jewish philosopher popular in the mid-20th Century, tells the story of a man who wanted to learn from a recognized mystical rabbi. He walks miles and miles to this master's town where he was known to give talks to anyone who was interested in listening. The student-to-be volunteers to serve the master, prepare his food, clean his house, etc. but never attends any of the master's public lectures. Someone asks him: "You came all this way to learn from the master, but you never attend his talks. Why not?" The man looks at him and answers, "I didn't come here to listen to the master talk. I came here to watch the master tie his shoes." (Sadiv, 2017. P 151).

If we want to know if someone has something of value to teach us, see what kind of life that person leads. Like children, we need to focus on what people do much more than what people say. If potential spiritual guides do not demonstrate some degree of harmony in their own lives, it is highly unlikely they will be able to help us achieve harmony in our own. And if that person wants to force that harmony to become ours as well, we had best run away.

8

The body/mind Dilemma

Descartes...before the horse?

When the French philosopher, Rene Descartes, declared "I think; therefore, I am!" in the 17th Century, he was taking a stand in a controversy that has existed throughout history. He thought he was establishing the foundation for the human ability to perceive what is "out there." In other words, how can anyone be certain about anything? Isn't it possible that everything is a delusion; that we are all locked away in some mental institution and the various experiences we think we are having are just figments of our imagination? For Descartes, the fact that people are able to think is conclusive proof that people exist and the universe—about which people think—is perceptible and real.

But just who/what are these "people"? Descartes maintained that individuals are essentially a combination of two distinct, but connected, entities: the spiritual mind and the physical body. This mind, or perhaps "soul," is eternal and indestructible. The body is constantly changing, growing and deteriorating over time. Exactly how the spiritual mind and the physical body are connected, and how that which is nonmaterial can control and/or be affected by the material, is a question that has not been satisfactorily answered to this day.

In this matter, Western religious traditions and Hinduism appear to agree. There is a spiritual soul (atman in Hinduism) that inhabits a physical body, to use Descartes' language, like a pilot controls a ship. The ultimate fate of this soul/atman is to return to the divine, whether to enjoy the pleasures of heaven in the Western religions or to somehow mystically reunify with the Brahman of Hinduism after a series of reincarnations.

While this mind/body dualism may seem self-evident, the Buddha rejected the idea of the existence of any permanent soul/atman. His doctrine, "anatta," maintained that there was no such permanent entity as a "soul/atman." For the Buddha, what appears as a "human being" is but a temporary coming together of five different qualities called "skandhas." These five are "form (the physical body), feelings, perceptions, thoughts, and awareness." One can quibble as to the distinctions between these attributes, but the important point is that they come together for a relatively short period of time and then, at death, they disassemble into their original, separate parts. The Buddha used the image of a house. A house seems like a "real" entity but, on closer examination, it is clear that it is composed of a number of component parts that will separate should the house be destroyed. There is no permanent "houseness" that inhabits these attributes. The house disappears when its parts separate.

It is this kind of reasoning that leads many atheistic science types to be sympathetic towards Buddhism. They, too, argue that there is no proof for any soul or atman and that what goes for "consciousness" is really just the by-product resulting from the various chemical and biological reactions of the physical body—reactions that will disappear once the host body disassembles at death. For them, there is no "ghost in the machine." That these scientists are demanding material proof for that which is immaterial is understandable, but not conclusive. After all, there are many scientific phenomena such as black holes and dark matter in which existence is inferred, but not measurable by any instruments presently available.

It is an important question that, if the Buddha's explanation is correct and there is no permanent soul/atman, just what is it that reincarnates after death? In fact, Buddhists take issue with the term *reincarnation* and its implication that there is "some thing"—a soul or atman or any other permanent essence—that changes forms from one life to the next much like a person changes clothes during his or her life. Still, Buddhists do believe that "something" continues after death and that the disintegration of the individual at death is not absolute. The issue is so amorphous, as it were, that there does not appear to be a term that precisely communicates what it is that Buddhists believe. Language like *rebirth* or the esoteric *metempsychosis* are used, but hardly helpful.

Maybe a better analogy to illustrate the Buddhist position is that of a river. A river exists, but it is not really an object. A river is constantly changing, "flowing." As they say, it is impossible to step into the same river twice. Further, a river flows from some source to some destination—a sea or an ocean. It isn't really possible to define with any precision exactly where, say the Mississippi River, ends and flows into the Gulf of Mexico. The distinction then, between the Mississippi River and the Gulf of Mexico, is not so distinct at all. Rather, the two appear to be part of the same water system. By the way, the same is true of the Gulf of Mexico and the Atlantic Ocean, in which case, there is also no clear distinction between the Mississippi River and the Atlantic Ocean, even though intuitively it seems like there should be.

The analogy works for Buddhists in that they see what might be called "psychic energy" in place of the water. It is this psychic energy that flows through time. This energy changes just like a river changes, depending on a variety of geological and geographic variables, and ultimately dissolves when it reaches its final destination. The waters status at different intervals can be identified for convenience sake, now a river, then an ocean, but these distinctions are fundamentally arbitrary in the strictest sense of the word. Buddhists would argue the same is true from one lifetime to the next: the psychic energy takes different forms depending on a variety of variables, but it would be misleading to claim there was something permanent that reincarnates in each lifetime.

Therefore, it seems that, theologically speaking, one must choose to believe in either the existence of a soul/atman or not. The quandary is common to personal experience. An adult has had a wide variety of personal experiences over time. Looking at different photographs taken during some of these experiences, one can see significant differences have taken place—physically, obviously, but also in terms of interests and intellectual and emotional development. In some ways, it seems clear that there is some unity throughout this personal history but, at the same time, this unity has somehow undergone constant changes. Western religions and Hinduism argue that it is the soul/atman that sustains this unity over time. Buddhism contends that the changes that take place over time take place with no need of any underlying, permanent soul/atman.

But maybe there is no need to choose between these two views. If there is a solution to this quandary, a clue may be found in one of the tenets of Quantum Physics. There it is said that, at the subatomic level, the same entity can display the characteristics of both a particle and a wave, depending on the conditions and whether that entity is being measured according to its speed or location. It is not that this entity is one or the other: it is both. It may very well be that the same is true of the human being; that the human being is not fundamentally either a "soul/atman" or a "river of energy" but, depending on the conditions and just what is being discussed—location or speed—the human being is fundamentally both simultaneously.

This is a definite problem in terms of formal, Aristotelian-type logic. 'A' equals 'A' and 'B' equals 'B.' 'A' does not equal 'B.' But this is not a problem at all in Taoism. In Taoism, "A" and "B" are not separate dualities. Rather, as in the Taoist symbol, "A" is "A" because of "B" and vice versa. For the Taoist, Descartes "body/soul" problem is only a problem because of a faulty focus on one isolated feature of reality—a reality that is more fully integrated that Descartes, writing in the classification-oriented West, could understand. The issue is linguistic only and, therefore, fictitious.

9

Eschatology

"Are we there yet?" (whatever..)

Theological discussions generally include questions about the nature of God, the existence of the soul, free will, and the like. If there are thoughts about history, they generally explore what is going to happen at the "End of Days" and whether there will be an ultimate Redemption—for the world's nations as a whole or individuals who have been brought back to life for eternal Judgment.

As important as these topics are, they invariably overlook a factor that seems critically important: just how long has history been taking place? For some that may be an insignificant, even silly question. After all, the universe as a whole is estimated to be about 14 billion years old—give or take. The earliest forms of life probably arose around 4 billion years ago, with humans appearing around 200,000 years ago. Recorded history does not take place until about 5,000 years ago with Sumerian cuneiform, roughly coinciding with Abraham in the Biblical *Book of Genesis.*

Given those kinds of numbers, it is fair to say that humans have been on the earth a very short period of time, relatively speaking. That is true. However, the assumption from the very start has been that the very existence of a Divine Intelligence can be inferred from the fact that there is a scientific orderliness in the universe that seems to require some kind of intent in order to be explained, the teleological argument. Further, as the *Bible* describes in its very first chapters, it seems that the ultimate goal of the scientific orderliness of the universe has something to do with humanity. It is only with the Creation of Mankind does the biblical God "rest." If that is the case, it is fair to ask: "If the point of Creation had something to do with Mankind, why did it take so long for Mankind to appear on the earth?" It seems that there were thousands and thousands and thousands of years invested in all kinds of mitochondria, dinosaurs, and a host of other life forms before humans appeared. It seems contrary to the spirit of teleology and God's omniscience to claim something along the lines that this was some kind of trial and error process. In fact, there are legends to the effect that there were any number of Creations before the Biblical one that God found unsatisfactory and destroyed in Noah-like fashion. Even so, the sheer amount of time involved seems quite inefficient at the very least, and such a grand scale of inefficiency seems hard to reconcile with the notion of a super-rational, teleological deity.

The same can be said if the focus is solely on human history. People have been around for 200,000 years, yet only the last 5,000 are actually recorded. One of the earliest models of Redemption comes from the Jewish tradition. The ancient Israelites were enslaved in Egypt for 400 years before Moses leads the exodus to the Promised Land, dated sometime around 1,300 BC or 3,300 years ago. That is a paradigm for redemption from slavery that is known the world over. Nevertheless, people seem to forget that it took 400 years to take place. That is a minuscule amount of time given the numbers of the age of the universe or the existence of humanity, Nevertheless, it means that in those 400 years there were 20 generations of people who were born, lived their lives and died as slaves before that Redemption. Even assuming that numbers like 400 or 20 are simply biblical jargon for "a lot"—the equivalent today of "I'll bet you a million dollars!"—it still means "a lot" of people suffered through slavery and never saw the benefits of the exodus.

The Jewish tradition also talks about the "End of Days" in which the Messiah comes to redeem the world as a whole. Exactly what that means is not that clear, but most accounts indicate that, at that time, all wars will cease, Jews from around the world will be brought back to Israel, the dead will be resurrected for eternal Judgment, and everyone will acknowledge that God is the one and only Lord of the Universe. For the Jews, despite centuries of prayers and declarations of "perfect faith in the coming of the Messiah," not only has that not happened yet, but there seems to be a tacit understanding that it is going to take a very long time, if it is going to happen at all. For example, in the Talmud there is the not-so-subtle advice to the effect that if you are planting a tree and someone tells you to rush to see because the Messiah has come, you should first finish planting your tree before you go to look—and the Talmud was completed around 1,700 years ago.

Of course, Christians will argue that the Messiah has, in fact, come to earth in the form of Jesus. However, the Hebrew prophecies regarding the Messianic Era were not met. Wars did not cease, Jews continued to suffer from Roman oppression, the dead were not resurrected, and any insistence that there was only one true Lord of the Universe was met with mocking laughter and much worse. There is reason to believe that there was every expectation that Jesus would return after the Crucifixion to overthrow the Roman authorities and fulfill the other Messianic requirements soon after. In fact, there are those who believe that was the reason for Judas's betrayal of Jesus; that the threat of Crucifixion would force Jesus's hand and cause the Redemption to take place. In any event, Jesus did return after the Crucifixion, but only for a few days and the other mandated requirements of the Messianic Era remain unfulfilled 2,000 plus years later.

Having said that, there is an intriguing alternative interpretation of what "the Messianic Era" means. "And when the Pharisees demanded when the kingdom of God should come, he answered them and said, 'The kingdom of God will not be seen. Neither shall they say, "It is here! or "It is there!" for, behold, the kingdom of God is within you.'" (Luke 17:20,21) In other words, the Messianic Era may not be some historical events that could be documented—the ending of wars or the migration of people—but is rather a frame of mind that is available for everyone every second of their lives.

Be that as it may, that same text continues with a vision of the apocalyptic "End of Days":

As it was in the days of Noe, so shall it be also in the days of the Son of Man. They ate, they drank, they married wives, they were given in marriage, until the day that Noah entered the ark, and the flood came and destroyed them all. Likewise, also as it was in the days of Lot; they ate, they drank, they bought, they sold, they planted, they built. But the same day that Lot went out of Sodom, it rained fire and brimstone from heaven and destroyed them all. Even thus shall it be in the day when the Son of man is revealed (Luke 17:27-30).

The two are not mutually exclusive. There may be a frame of mind in which people at any time can experience the Kingdom of Heaven that is perpetually in their hearts. However, that does not preclude the dogma that there will be an extraordinary historical event in keeping with the Jewish tradition.

Finally, Islam, the third of the monotheistic religions, has a similar eschatology. While Muhammed was a human prophet and not theologically comparable to a Jesus who was both fully human and divine, in Islam Muhammed was also the last and greatest prophet. That suggests that there was nothing especially new that Allah had to reveal following the death of Muhammed in 632 AD. There is no anticipated Second Coming of Muhammed, but there is to be a horrific Armageddon after which the dead will be brought back to life for eternal Judgment. The good will be forever rewarded with all the pleasures of heaven while the evil will suffer all the torments of hell. Again, that was prophesied about 1500 years ago. As such, it is difficult to understand why so much time has passed before the Islamic version of the "End of Days."

Therefore, Jews, Christians, and Muslims alike all agree there will be some kind of Messianic Era that will take place at the end of time. There are differences of opinion regarding details, but there seems to be a consensus there will be an Armageddon followed by a Judgment Day in which the fates of the righteous and unrighteous will be determined for all eternity. That the Judgment Day has been so long in coming is recognized, but never really resolved.

Eastern religions like Taoism, Hinduism and Buddhism avoid the problem altogether because they have no eschatology. It is true that Taoists talk of creation in the sense that the Tao emanates the yin and yang, the primary duality, which then emanates "all the things of all reality" (Lao Tzu, 1:2), but it would be a mistake to see that as comparable to the *Genesis* account, "In the beginning, God created the heavens and the earth" (Gen. 1:1) because it suggests a chronology—a before and after that is not present in Taoism. If anything, rather eerily, Taoists agree with ancient Greek philosophers like Aristotle and modern astrophysicists in that the universe is seen as eternal. The point is more subtle than "the universe has always existed." Rather, as time is the measurement of motion, time itself came into existence with the universe of things that move. That seems counter-intuitive. After all, what would it mean to use language like "came into existence"? It is such a quandary posed by trying to use language regarding such topics that caused the Buddha to dismiss the entire discussion as meaningless and a distraction from the real issues of human suffering that need addressing.

Hinduism, though, takes the question very seriously. They posit that the universe is eternal in the same sense as above, with time itself coming into existence with the universe. How long has the universe been around? Hindus say that the history of the universe includes a series of expansions and contractions called *kalpas,* each of which took about 4 or 5 billion years. And how many kalpas have there been since the beginning of time. Depending on who is doing the counting, there have been approximately 36,000 kalpas, give or take. This timeline does suggest comparisons with the scientific idea that this present universe began with the "Big Bang" some 14 billion years ago and will contract again to that irreducibly dense dot in another 5 billion years.

Compare that with Bishop Ussher's assertion in the 17th Century. By taking the various chronologies in the Bible, the 7 days of Creation and the lives and deaths of all the biblical personalities, he said the universe is about 7,000 years old. As Joseph Campbell, author of *The Hero with a Thousand Faces* and popularizer of mythological paradigms from around the world, observed, it is unfortunate that Western religions adopted such a limited timeline when trying to explain the antiquity of the universe. Of course, technically it can be argued that the biblical case is not so simple as the sun, moon and stars were only created on the fourth day of Creation. Therefore, as with the Taoists and astrophysicists, there is no way of knowing just how long those first three "days" may have been.

That is fair, but really beside the point. Whether or not there was a beginning or how that beginning can be understood, the real issue is whether there will be an end. Judaism, Christianity and Islam all seem to agree that there will be an "end"—a culmination of history that will ultimately validate that history as a vindication of that religion's belief system. Frankly, given how much time has passed, that is reminiscent of *Waiting for Godot*; we may wait expectantly as long as we like but, at the end of the day, as it were, Godot never arrives.

10

Reincarnation

"You can check out any time you like, but you can never leave." (The Eagles)

Voltaire was an 18th-century French playwright and skeptic. Suffice it to say he did not have kind things to say about religion in general and the Catholic Church in particular. He is probably best known for *Candide*, a play about a naive young man who believes his tutor, Dr. Pangloss, who steadfastly asserts that "This is the best of all possible worlds." Alas, Candide falls prey to any number of miscreants and comical tragedies, well, comical to the audience at least, and he begins to doubt that Pangloss's teachings reflect the reality of his experience (1759, https//gutenberg.org).

Martin accompanies Candide on his travels and at one point Candide sighs:

Do you believe,,, that men have always massacred each other as they do today; that they have always been liars, cheats, traitors, ingrates, brigands, idiots, thieves, scoundrels, gluttons, drunkards, misers, envious, ambitious, bloody-minded, calumniators, debauchees, fanatics, hypocrites, and fools? (1759, p. 105).

Martin gazes at his good, if all too simple, companion. "'Do you believe,' said Martin, 'that hawks have always eaten pigeons when they have found them?'" (1759. p. 104,).

If the Buddha taught that we should only believe that which makes sense to us, rejecting even his own teachings if they do not, then one way we can determine what makes sense to us is by comparing our experiences with what teachers are teaching. In the context of theology, essentially two world views are proclaimed:

1) The Western religious view is that God created this world as something of a testing ground to distinguish those who are good from those who are evil. Those who are good are eternally rewarded in heaven and those who are evil are eternally punished in Hell.

2) The Eastern religious view that there is a mysterious Divine Intelligence (DI) responsible for a universe in which individuals strive, usually after many lifetimes, to dispel the illusions of separation and reunite with that "Divine Intelligence."

The Western religious view is pretty straightforward and has an appearance of justice—therefore affirming the assumption that "God is good" and that God cares. After all, it is only fair that good people should be rewarded and evil people should be punished. In terms of historical experience, it is true that the good often suffer and that the evil often prosper, but that is just a temporary situation. In fact, that is the test itself. If it was obvious that following the good leads to prosperity, there would be no real choice to be tested. There can only be faith where there is room for doubt.

That is the direct message of the Biblical *Book of Job.* Job is by all accounts a God-fearing man who does all the good things God-fearing men do. "He fears God and stays away from evil" (*Job* 2:3). When God tells Satan about the potential good of humanity, God points to Job as a prime example of what everyone can ideally become. Satan scoffs: "Skin for skin! Certainly, a man will give everything he has for his life. But stretch out your hand and strike his flesh and bones. I bet he'll curse you to your face" (*Job* 2:4-5). God then allows Satan to test Job. To determine the depth of Job's faith, Satan has him afflicted with all kinds of horrible diseases. His wife and children are murdered and he loses all his possessions. Though he is bewildered, telling his friends that he could not have done anything so terrible to merit such a dreadful fate, "Job's lips never uttered a sinful word." Ultimately Job's steadfast faith is rewarded. His health is restored, he remarries and has more children, and he regains his lost riches.

The *Book of Job* thus appears to be a clear vindication of God's goodness and the validity of suffering as a test of human faith. Of course, it is true that not every good person gains personal happiness and material wealth during this lifetime. Not every good person has a Job-like happy ending. Again, if everyone could see that every good person has a Job-like happy ending, there would be no temptation to sin. That is what heaven is for: to provide the reward once the test is over and has been passed. As Utah Phillips smirks in his song, "The Preacher and the Slave," "There'll be pie in the sky when you die" (2011).

On closer examination, though, the message of the *Book of Job* is not so clear. While the usual popular debate about the Book is whether God was cruel to allow Satan to afflict the innocent Job like that, no one seems to pay any attention to Job's wife and children. While they may not have been as perfectly God-fearing as Job, they were, in fact, killed through no apparent fault of their own. It is possible that they were rewarded in heaven, but there is the nagging thought that they got there by default. They come across as the collateral damage of God's wager with Satan about Job. That there is collateral damage in real life for all kinds of worthy endeavors is certainly true, but it hardly seems "fair" from a divine point of view.

But besides the *Book of Job,* the fundamental assumption is that "This is it!" Everyone has one life and, depending on one's conduct in this one and only life, one will merit eternal reward or damnation. However, if that is the test for everyone, shouldn't everyone have the same test? People are born, live and die under all kinds of circumstances. How is it fair to evaluate the conduct of a 6-year-old peasant child who died in the Middle Ages with that of, say, a Hugh Hefner who died at 91 after having parlayed *Playboy Magazine* into a multi-billion dollar financial enterprise along with considerable "business with benefits?" That may seem like an extreme example, but similar comparisons can be made regarding those who die every single day of every single year, of all races, creeds, ages, financial situations, geographical locations, with and without parents, etc. In fact, Western monotheistic religious scholars must wrestle with the question as to the fate of all those who died either before the revelation of the one true faith or lived in ignorance of it. It seems very logical, if uncomfortable, to assume that if faith in the one and only God is a prerequisite for admittance into heaven, the reason for not having that faith is irrelevant.

It appears that the faithful themselves may have doubts along these lines. For example, there are tales where older sinners condemned to Hell plead that it was not their fault that they lived so long and had to face so many more opportunities to sin than those who died at much younger ages, even as children. And then there are caveats regarding the mentally ill. Suicide, for instance, is a heinous sin and those who kill themselves cannot usually be buried in the religion's cemeteries and are presumed rejected from heaven. However, if the individual is determined to have been depressed, mentally ill or deficient, the assumption is that the suicide was a symptom of psychological distress and, therefore, the individual could not be held accountable.

Assuming DI is all-powerful and cares about people, it seems terribly arbitrary and unjust to judge individuals of myriad variables according to one identical standard. There simply must be a better, fairer way to determine a person's fate for all eternity. Consider the human model of, say, Contract Bridge. In these card-playing tournaments, the teams rotate from table to table with each having the opportunity to play the exact hand, the "contract." The luck of the draw is thus minimized and the skill of the teams can be more fairly determined through the competition. Chess is another example. Players start from the same, equal positions and devise their own plans and strategies, with the results determined by the various skills of the players.

In either of these examples, the players are not entirely and always equal. They all are born with different talents and different players have different levels of preparation and different psychological energies. Nevertheless, the rules are the same for everyone and everyone has the opportunity to make their own free choices regarding how to play the game, with results determined by the quality of play.

This analogy of this life, not being a one-time test, but a game is indicative of the basic world view of Hinduism when it comes to reincarnation. While not nearly so well known, there are actually mystics in just about every religious tradition who also believe in reincarnation. In Judaism, the tradition of the Kabbalah maintains there is the *gilgul nefashot* (the circle of souls) and there are similar minority views of those like Origen in early Christianity or the Sufis in Islam. There is also the assumption of some form of reincarnation in Taoism and Buddhism, but only in Hinduism is the doctrine explicitly part of the mainline teachings and expressed in considerable detail.

The Hindu context for reincarnation is important to understand. To summarize, Brahman is infinite and there was only Brahman. After all, if one is "infinite," how can there be room for anything else? However, a static infinity can be characterized as infinitely boring, so Brahman separated Himself in all the various features of the universe, human, animal, material, etc. "This whole universe is Brahman. In tranquility, let one worship It, as *Taj Jalan* (that from which he came forth, as that into which he will be dissolved, as that in which he breathes)" (Upanishads). In that way, Brahman can experience an infinite number of perspectives, much like people read novels or watch movies which allow access to any number of personalities, time periods, and locations.

In terms of the "game," every individual has an atman (soul) which is actually part of Brahman, a part that appears to be separate, but actually is not. The image is often given of waves relative to the ocean or cells in a body. They appear to be separate, but that separation is only an illusion, *maya*. The goal of the game is to dispel the illusion and consciously reestablish the unity with the divine, a sort of eternal game of hide-and-seek that, once achieved, spiritual types call enlightenment (*moksha*).

As with Shakespeare's "All the world's a stage," in Hinduism, Brahman takes the form of people who play all the roles throughout time in this historical, cosmic drama. There are good guys, but for there to be drama there have to be bad guys as well—and luck and sadness and tragedy and success and love and bitter rivalries and any number of surprises. As Alan Watts observes, at the end of every good show the audience applauds for the bad guys as well as the good as they realize that, without their excellent performance, the show would not be successful (1965). Imagine a theatrical show where everyone gets along, loves one another and enjoys peace and tranquility in scene after scene in some idyllic, pastoral setting like, say, the Garden of Eden. Suffice it to say that it will not be long before the audience starts trickling out of the auditorium and, with the infinity of time at Brahman's disposal, the question becomes, "Now what?" In Hinduism, as with any game or show, the answer is simple: you put the pieces and costumes away for a while and then you start all over again.

At this point, the objection can be raised that this whole scenario trivializes the human experience and especially all its pervasive suffering. The theater, chess games—they are fine in and of themselves, but they are not real. It is one thing to see a child die on the screen. It is quite another to hold one's own child as s/he dies in one's arms.

True enough. There is the Taoist point that the ability to love a child must be related to the sensitivity to the possibility of suffering, but that is a different context. In Hinduism, the power of the theater lies in the ability to "suspend belief." In other words, if one constantly remembers, or is annoyingly constantly reminded, "What's the big deal; it's only a movie," then the whole experience is ruined. The ability to appreciate a performance is proportionate to the ability to empathize and identify with characters being portrayed. The more real the action seems to be, the more effective the show.

If that seems heartless, remember that the show, all shows, are temporary. There comes a time when the curtain goes down and comes back up—with the audience applauding as the actors take their bows. That is obvious when it comes to shows on a stage. In Hinduism, that is the case in real life as well.

Of course, that raises the question as to just what the term *real* means. In the West, there seems to be some kind of absolute quality that establishes some absolute meaning to what happens in life, whether joyful or tragic. Nevertheless, if there is an eternity awaiting everyone in heaven or hell, there, too, "what happens in life" is also temporary and, as indicated above, rather arbitrary, given the infinite variety of our "one and only" lifetimes.

The Hindu approach, "For the soul, there is never birth nor death. Nor, having once been, does he ever cease to be. He is unborn, eternal, ever-existing, undying and primeval. He is not slain when the body is slain not" (Bhagavad Gita, 2:19-20), not only makes more sense, but it is also more consistent with the supposition that DI is all-powerful and all caring. That does not minimize the joy nor the anguish people experience in this reality. People feel what they feel, but then there is a different perspective.

Just about every adult can remember a childhood experience that was terribly painful and seemed like it would last forever. Sometimes it took an hour and sometimes it took months or years, but eventually the adult reached the point where that childhood experience became a memory, a formative experience that left significant scars, but still a memory so that the adult could move on and live a life of different experiences. That is the essence of the Hindu idea of "enlightenment:" the experiences themselves were experienced as real, but the perspective on those experiences changes with time and maturity.

But if the Hindu approach that all that exists is a matter of divine entertainment is too unsettling as it may diminish the significance of suffering and pain in life, then consider what lessons may be learned from the Crucifixion of Jesus. The agony of the Passion of Jesus is unquestionable and at the very end, maybe mercifully, comes death itself. But while not the same as reincarnation, Jesus does not come back to life in some other form or identity, Jesus is resurrected in a way that is somehow recognizable by those who were devoted to him. Jesus clearly appears to have died, but yet has not.

This paradox may be the key to understanding the verse, "Then Jesus told His disciples, 'If anyone wants to come after Me, he must deny himself and take up his cross and follow Me; *for whoever wants to save his life will lose it, but whoever loses his life for My sake will find it'"* (*Matthew* 16:24-25). In other words, one whose mindset is restricted to the physical life and devotes all his energies to continuing the physical life is doomed to fail as the physical life is doomed to die. However, "something" continues after, that "something" usually construed as something spiritual, and to the degree that one identifies with that mysterious "something," one is guaranteed eternal life, whatever mysterious form that may take. It is similar to Jesus commanding Peter to follow him and walk on the water. Initially, Peter focuses on Jesus and begins to do so, "But when he saw the wind, he was afraid and, beginning to sink, cried out, 'Lord, save me!' Immediately Jesus reached out his hand and caught him. 'You of little faith,' he said, "why did you doubt?'" (*Matthew* 14: 30-31).

The question that goes unasked is just how was Peter able to walk on the water initially and did he need Jesus to save him from drowning. The traditional understanding is that Peter walked on the water by virtue of Jesus's power and that ultimately Jesus saved him from drowning because Peter's fear of the wind was more significant to him than his faith in Jesus. But suppose the real message is that Peter could walk on the water himself? Suppose his doubt was about his own identity as someone vulnerable to physical forces of nature and not, as Jesus was attempting to teach him, as someone endowed with "something" that meant that walking on the water, or even death itself, was...well...immaterial?

Viewed this way, there is very little difference between the Hindu experience of "enlightenment" and the Christian experience of being "born again." In both cases, the physical limitations of life have been superseded by a more accurate perception of what the individual is and how the individual relates to what is perceived as physical reality. In both cases death itself loses its power because that "something" is beyond its grasp.

11

Why be good?

"When I'm good, I'm very good; but when I'm bad, I'm better." (Mae West)

Given the context of religious world views, a natural question is "why be good?" While the quote "Eat, drink and be merry" is well known, the unpleasant rejoinder "for tomorrow we die" is far less popular. That does not necessarily mean there should be unbounded hedonism. Yes, there was the rather common practice of the Epicureans in ancient Greece of eating so much and then forcing oneself to throw up so as to be able to continue indulging. (To this day, the term *epicurean* means "one who is a connoisseur of the various pleasures life has to offer.") The truth is that immoderate pleasure generally leads to consequences that are most unpleasant. In any event, for such individuals the goal remains "pleasure" itself as the same fate for eternal darkness awaits everyone. It is only a matter of how to most efficiently enjoy oneself, not whether such enjoyment should be the ultimate goal.

The Biblical "Parable of the Rich Fool" recognizes the appeal of this viewpoint. Here a wealthy man has accumulated a great many riches and is actively planning to acquire more land and all the prestige that goes with it—only to have God inform him, "Fool! Tonight your soul is required of you, and the things you have prepared, whose will they be?'" (Luke 12:20) In other words, there may be those who believe there is no metaphysical purpose to life and, since lifetimes are limited, it is best to enjoy what time there is as best we can. However, there should be no illusion that there is any long term security purchased along with those acquisitions.

But suppose one does have a metaphysical outlook and believes there may be more after death than "eternal darkness." The Western monotheistic world views, with their promises of heaven, would seem to provide the best Epicurean answer. After all, what could be better than the eternal pleasures of heaven? From an Epicurean perspective, the Islamic descriptions of the heavenly rewards for good behavior in this life may be the most persuasive. For example: "Those will have gardens of perpetual residence; beneath them rivers will flow. They will be adorned therein with bracelets of gold and will wear green garments of fine silk and brocade, reclining therein on adorned couches. Excellent is the reward, and good is the resting place" (*Koran* 18:31).

It is interesting that so many of the Koran's depictions of heaven have to do with gardens and water, no doubt due to the arid climates of Saudi Arabia and North Africa where Islam initially spread. More relevant may be a possible interpretation of "Whenever they are provided with a provision of fruit therefrom, they will say, 'This is what we were provided with before.' And it is given to them in likeness" (*Koran* 2:25). This phrasing suggests that those who live good lives will be rewarded in heaven in a manner with which they are already familiar: "what we were provided with before." In that sense, gardens and water make perfect sense for Muslims who lived their lives in and around deserts. Muslims who lived their lives in and around the rain forests of Indonesia, surprisingly, the country with the most Muslims in the world, might envision a different Paradise.

In any event, if the appropriate reward for good behavior is an Epicurean satisfaction of the physical senses, these Islamic images would be hard to beat. Having said that, there is also the possibility that rewards are not necessary for good behavior. For example, there is the Jewish Talmudic teaching:

Antigonus of Sokcho received the teaching from Shimon the Righteous. He used to say: "Do not be as servants who serve the Master to receive a reward. Rather, be as servants who serve the Master not to receive a reward. And let the fear of heaven be upon you" (Ethics of the Fathers 1:3).

Rather than Epicurean and sensual, the nature of the reward may be more spiritual. As it says in the Talmud, "The World to Come, *Olam Haba*, is where the soul basks in the radiance of God's glory (*Berachot*. 17a)." In fact, the reward may not have anything to do with heaven at all. In the "Ethics of the Father," the rabbis teach: "Better is one hour of repentance and good deeds in this world than the whole life of the World to Come; and better is one hour of bliss in the World-to-Come than the whole life of this world" (*Ethics* 4:17).

Jesus has a similar teaching in that "The Kingdom of Heaven is within you" (*Luke* 17:21). In other words, the "reward" may be a frame of mind, a sense of contentment and equanimity, perhaps, that is attainable in this world as well as in the world to come. Consider another of Jesus's teachings: "Look at the birds. They don't plant or harvest or store food in barns, for your heavenly Father feeds them. And aren't you far more valuable to him than they are?" (*Matthew* 6:26) On one level the text seems to be saying that God will not let the faithful go hungry just as he does not let the birds in the skies go hungry. That, however, is obviously not true as birds not only go hungry on occasion; rather, some birds actually eat other birds. On the other hand, if the verse is referring to a state of mind in which birds do what birds do without anxiety, whether eating or being eaten, then there is an equanimity that goes with that acceptance. Note that this does not mean that birds do not experience fear. It is that birds and all animals accept that fear itself. Fear causes them to flee from an enemy but, should the escape prove successful, it disappears. Anxiety seems to be a quality that may be uniquely human. In that sense, equanimity in the face of whatever happens may be interpreted as a reward for faith.

The Hindu concept of reincarnation is essentially different. As opposed to a reward for good behavior or punishment for bad behavior, the reward or punishment is possibly different depending on the tastes and personality of the individual, as indicated previously. Hindus believe that everyone will eventually come to the same place, a reunification with the Brahman who started the entire process. Progress is measured by the degree to which an individual recognizes that s/he is fundamentally not an "individual" at all, but rather a part of a divine whole. Seen this way, karma is not a process of reward and punishment, but an instructional tool.

While Buddhism generally discourages such metaphysical speculations, the idea that there can be either an immediate or eventual realization that "all is one" is an essential element of Buddhist teachings. Compassion in Buddhism is not the result of some saintly self-sacrifice that one performs to benefit others. Rather, the enlightened Buddhist recognizes the unity of all life and, while probably misleading to put it in such terms, recognizes that by helping others s/he is helping his/herself at the same time. For example, in the body, the foot may be in pain, but the hand is not jealous of the attention that is devoted to healing the foot. If it could be conscious, the hand would recognize that healing the foot contributes to the wellbeing of the entire body, which includes the hand.

That leads to the Zen Buddhist notion of a "bodhisattva." This is an individual who is enlightened and could enter nirvana—a state in which the cycle of life and death is extinguished because the reality has been realized—but refuses to do so until everyone can be assisted to reach the same state. It is reminiscent of those African athletes at the Olympics who confounded the authorities when, at the end of the race, the winner refused to cross the finish line until all the other competitors caught up so as not to embarrass them.

Similarly, Taoists believe there is behavior that is consistent with the Tao and behavior which is not. It is misleading to say that behavior consistent with the Tao is rewarded by success or that behavior inconsistent with the Tao is punished by failure. One who does not jump off a cliff is not rewarded by staying alive or, if s/he does jump, is not punished by crashing to death.

Terms like *reward* and *punishment* in the West suggest some authority who decides on standards of behavior and doles out the just results. In the East, the imagery is closer to that of natural law. Whether the terminology is of karma or compassion or the Tao, reality operates according to certain principles and one violates those principles at considerable risk.

12

The Individual on Trial

"Ask not for whom the bell tolls. It tolls for thee."
(Dunne)

At this point it makes sense to summarize the key elements of this "theology for the rest of us":

1) The orderliness of the universe indicates the presence of a divine intelligence (DI) responsible for that orderliness. This DI is conscious and cares.

2) DI is all-powerful, but that only refers to that which is possible. Even DI cannot add 2 + 2 and get 3.

3) Everything in the universe is subject to change. It is this potential for change that allows for the opening of free will.

4) "Free will" exists, and the question itself presumes its existence.

5) While terribly risky, free will is essential to human dignity and spirituality, and another sign that DI cares. Like a parent with a child, DI is willing to allow people to learn from their experiences and further their development.

6) Teachers can be helpful, but they must not insist on a cult-like following.

7) Humans are not bodies or souls, but bodies and souls—more like flowing rivers than fixed entities.

8) The duration of human history makes an end of days or final messianic era improbable.

9) Assuming DI exists, cares and is powerful, reincarnation is necessary to allow for an even playing field for individuals. Without reincarnation, there is no level playing field for the infinite variety of individual circumstances.

10) People should behave morally not out of any expectation of reward or fear of punishment, but as a reflection of the understanding that "all is one."

These 10 precepts, though definitely not commandments, can form the basis of a reasonably coherent theology that can reassure any skeptical individual who is anxious about his or her own rationality. There is nothing weird here or anything antithetical to scientific reasoning. As such, it can provide the grounding that may allow the individual to give him or herself permission to consider the possibilities involved in a metaphysical, theological realm. This permission may be absolutely necessary for those who are worried about being "kooks" or even insane. That is not to say that these beliefs will lead to social acceptance. For whatever reason—maybe their own doubts or insecurities—-people may very well reject individuals who do not conform to the accepted mores and beliefs. That those accepted mores and beliefs are labeled religious is misleading at best as they do not allow the kind of personal freedom that is essential to true spirituality. It is possible that such social rejection will lead the questioning individual to other kindred spirits and form a new social community, but there is no guarantee. Nevertheless, the alternative of squelching one's spiritual aspirations for the sake of social acceptance cannot be preferable or even healthy. Once those thoughts and feelings begin to emerge, they cannot be repressed without significant damage.

With this kind of rational assurance, it is possible that the seeker can now be open to what may be termed "truly spiritual experiences." For example, consider the story of Jacob's Ladder in Chapter 28 of the biblical *Book of Genesis*. It is the middle of the night. Jacob is all by himself in the middle of nowhere. He is terrified of the prospect of meeting his brother, Esau, the next day. Esau may very well be plotting his deadly revenge as Jacob can be accused of stealing his birthright and paternal blessing. The area is so barren he needs to use a rock as his pillow. Nevertheless, it is in this dire situation that Jacob has a dream in which he envisions angels ascending and descending on a ladder stretching from heaven to earth. At the very top is God Himself who renews His covenant that Jacob's "descendants will be like the dust of the earth" and will accompany Jacob wherever he goes. Jacob is awestruck. "When Jacob awoke from his sleep, he thought, 'Surely the LORD is in this place, and I was not aware of it'" (*Gen* 28:16).

How many people may experience the very same awe at the myriad wonders of the universe if they would just allow themselves to be open to it? It may be similar to the vulnerability necessary to truly experience love. One cannot be guarded and at the same time give oneself to another. Is there a great risk of such openness? Perhaps, and yet it is important to remember that there is great risk of not having such openness. Exactly what has been the value of a life that, however lengthy, has been lived without love? Socrates is supposed to have said, "The unexamined life is not worth living." Maybe the same is true about a life without love, or a deep appreciation of just how marvelous the universe really is.

It is intriguing that so many mystics talk about "love" in the context of their experiences of the divine. Rumi, the Persian 13th-century poet, joins with a great many mystics in all religious traditions when he says "Without *love* I was one who had lost the way; all of a sudden *love* entered. I was a mountain; I became straw for the horse of the king" Rumi, 2009, p. 24). Alfred Lord Tennyson (1850) is likely quite right when he says "Tis better to have loved and lost than to have never loved at all." However, how much better, and safer, is it to love with the assurance that that love will be requited by the divine love inherent in all of reality.

But suppose we are not there yet. Suppose, whether because of our rationality or in spite of it, we just do not feel either love or awe. After all, the field is called "metaphysics" because it is "beyond the physical." Suppose we are on this side of the door and have no idea as to what is on the other side. The door seems locked to us, so what is the possible alternative to just going about our business until somebody else opens the door? This is indeed a sad state of affairs, and one in which the overwhelming majority of the rest of us find ourselves. As Rumi sighs, "Take an axe to dig through the prison; you will all be kings and princes!" (Rumi, 2009, p. 86)

Having said that, there may be an alternative approach. Assuming we are in prison and have not yet realized we have the key, maybe we can still experience some of the benefits of the spiritual life. People like the 17th-century French mathematician Blaise Pascal and the 20th Century American psychologist William James have offered a sort of "cost benefit analysis" of faith in God. Given the ineffable nature of God, assume that it is impossible to know for sure whether or not God exists. Suppose one believes in God and it turns out God does not exist. Now suppose that one does not believe in God, but God does exist. In which scenario do we experience greater benefits? In which scenario do we risk greater losses? By benefits and losses, the intent is not about the possibility of heavenly reward or eternal damnation, though those possibilities are necessarily included, but rather which scenario is more likely to lead to a more appreciative, grateful life, a life more likely to bring one happiness and contentment? Surely there is more hope for happiness and contentment with a worldview that sees life as an integral, ongoing part of the consciousness of reality, surviving even death, as opposed to a worldview that sees death as the annihilation of any conscious life on an individual basis and ultimately of any and all consciousness.

As clear as that choice may be, again, given the impossibility of knowing for sure either way, there may still be some reluctance. Perhaps that reluctance has to do with all the associations, whether conscious or unconscious, with the term "God." Suppose instead that the choice was articulated along these lines: "Given the impossibility of knowing for sure, is it better for an individual to believe in the orderliness of the entire universe than to believe that all reality is fundamentally chaotic?" Most would agree that some belief in the orderliness of the universe not only has more potential for happiness and contentment, but for sheer sanity as well. If so, there is little point in quibbling over whether there is a God who is responsible for that orderliness, even if the latter logically suggests the former.

Having said that, ultimately happiness is indeed a choice. Again, given the lack of absolute information, believing in the orderliness of the universe is more likely to lead to happiness than the alternative. However, another factor of happiness has to do with authenticity. In other words, for people to be happy, there has to be integrity in the sense that what one does is an expression of what one believes. That is a lot more difficult than it sounds. As the 20th-century, French existentialist Jean Paul Sartre says in his play, *No Exit*, "Hell is other people" (1943, p. 45). There are extraordinary pressures to conform to what others in society consider good and acceptable. Worse, as these pressures have been applied since birth, they generally have become internalized so that there can be extraordinary fear, anxiety and shame attached to thinking and feeling outside these social norms. Nevertheless, if what is unique about the individual is suppressed in order to appease others, the resulting tension leads to everything but happiness.

There is a very special Jewish Hasidic story about Zusya, a poor man on his death bed. Besides his physical condition, Zusya was terribly agitated. A rabbi was called to comfort him. When the rabbi asked Zusya what was troubling him, Zusya answered, "I am afraid. I have lived a pretty good life....not perfect, but pretty good. Still, I was no Moses. I am afraid that they will not let me into heaven because I was not good enough." The rabbi took Zusya's hand in his and said, "Do not worry. When you approach heaven, they will not ask you why you were not Moses. They will ask you why you were not Zusya."

At the beginning of this book, we imagined entering a large dark room, filled with fancy set tables and chairs. There was a long dais at the front with more chairs and a podium with a microphone. At the time, the question was whether all that got there by accident, randomly thrown into the room by some thieves or maybe movers for storage, or whether all that got there because someone planned it that way, plausibly for some kind of banquet. The idea that all that got there by accident seemed more than implausible, even though the one who did the planning was never actually seen. The point was that, if such a hall could not have been the result of some accident, there was no way the entire universe, with all its intricate laws and patterns, could have been the result of some accident, either. If so, there must be a "Divine Intelligence," DI, operating in some fashion that is responsible for the universe.

Now imagine that, on leaving that hall, you see a sign by the door. You reasonably assume that the sign will give you a clue as to the honoree of the celebration. When you look more closely, you see that your very own name appears.

Once you get over the shock and awe, the questions come quickly. What are you going to say? How honest will you be? Will you just talk about your successes...or will you be forthcoming about not only your failures, but your regrets? What would you hope others would say? Those others might be loved ones who will be caring and forgiving, but they might be enemies, too. Will they admit they respected you even though they bitterly fought against you? What about your mentors, those people who recognized your potential and helped you along the way? Will they be proud of what you've done? Or will there be just a hint of "S/he could have been one of the very best, but..."?

Will there be a Questions and Answers session? What will people ask? "When were you happiest?" "How did you get the idea to get started on your life's work?" "What was the hardest thing you ever did?" "Is there anything you would have done differently?" "What advice do you have for those who will come after you?" And maybe the most important question of all: Looking back over all of it, were you truly you?

Technically speaking, *theology* is about defining and understanding what is "out there." Who/What is responsible for this reality in which we find ourselves? Fundamentally, though, theology is about how we relate to the

Who/What responsible for this reality in which we find ourselves. It is about honesty, authenticity, and the realization that, because there is some DI responsible for this reality in which we find ourselves, it will all be ok.

Finally, in this context, you may be wondering: "Just who is this 'we' in which 'we' find 'ourselves in this reality? For that matter, who is the "us" in "a theology for the rest of us"? After all, if theology is so personal and individual, how can there ever be a meaningful "we" or "us"?

That is an important question, especially in this particular reality in which we find ourselves. Everything is so polarized in so many areas. Everything is all too often classified into "us" and "them": "you're either for us or agin' us." People who disagree are not simply "mistaken" or even "wrong;" they are "stupid" or, worse, "evil." The notion that different people can have different legitimate opinions—that different, even apparently contradictory, opinions can each be "right" simultaneously, depending on the context and circumstances of those different people—is a notion that inspires skepticism and charges of treason. Even agreement can be suspect unless it is 100% and refuses to acknowledge that the "other" may have some points worth considering.

There is a famous parable found in many traditions of a group of blind men who come across an elephant. Each is in contact with a different part of the animal and draws conclusions accordingly. So, for example, the one holding the tail assumes the elephant is snake-like. The one touching a tusk decides the elephant must be made of stone. A third cannot reach around the leg and claims the elephant is like a huge tree. The argument goes on and on until, in most versions, the group of blind men separate with each thinking the others are close-minded, sadly mistaken, and worse. Of course, each blind man was telling the truth in the sense there was no intent to deceive, but that "truth" was only partial—substantial enough to appear credible, but not nearly complete.

The usual point of the parable is to show how our perceptions are invariably limited and how much everyone has potentially to gain from sharing information and being open to different perspectives. That is the attitude of the "us" in "a theology for the rest of us." We are all individuals who, like Zusya, strive to be honest and authentic. However, we acknowledge that we have no monopoly on "the TRUTH;" that we can learn much more by sharing what we have learned as individuals instead of by insisting we have already learned all there is to learn. This recognition may have been what Jesus had in mind when he taught: "First remove the beam from your own eye, and then you will see clearly enough to remove the speck from your brother's eye." (*Matthew* 7:5) This is not an easy approach to adopt—particularly in a world that preaches independence and individuality, just so long as you think and act just like all the right people.

Of course, all this questioning and exploring and even arguing are all part of the process. As Richard Bach says in his novel, *Illusions,* "Here is a test to find whether your mission on earth is finished: If you are still alive, you haven't." (1977, p. 158). If we already know all the answers, why bother with exploring? Yes, it is often difficult and confusing and lonely—often desperately lonely. It is so much easier—safer—to be absolutely sure; to neatly fit into a category where one can find acceptance in conformity. But, again, once we believe that DI not only exists, but also cares about us, we can be confident as to our ultimate success.

In the meantime, we can only do our best—and cherish the company of those kindred spirits around us along our way.

References

Asar. (2019) *Are all things good and evil from Allah?* http://www.asaratthedesk.com/2019/02/10/thing-good-evil-allah/

Bach, R. (1977). *Illusions.* NY: Dell.

Bhagavad Gita as it s. (1972) *https://www.asitis.com/*

Bjordal, M. (2020). *Kisa Gotami and the parable of the mustard seed.* (http://www.allcreation.org/home/kisa-gotami)

Born, M. (2004) *The Born-Einstein Letters, 1916-55)* London: Palgrave-McMillan

Cameron, J. (1984) *The Terminator.* Orion Pictures

Carus, P. (1894) *The Gospel of Buddha.* (http://www.mountainman.com.au/buddha/carus_93.htm)

DeChardin, P. T. (1946). *The Future of man.* Downloaded December 28, 2020 from https://b-ok.cc/book/3619795/59e8d1.

Dostoyevsky, F. (1880) *The Brothers Karamazov.* Downloaded December 28, 2020 from https://www.gutenberg.org/files/28054/28054-pdf.pdf.

Dostoyevsky, F. (1866/1992). *Crime and punishment.* NY: Alfred A. Knopf, Inc.

Edwards, J. (1741). *Sinners in the hands of an angry God.* Downloaded December 28, 2020 from https://digitalcommons.unl.edu/etas/54/.

Gervitz, G. (1995) *Partners with God.* Springfield, NJ: Berman House.

*Gospel of Thomas.*http://www.earlychristianwritings.com/thomas/gospelthomas3.html

Hunt, J. *Alan Watts on the 5 most important lessons for the 21st Century. https://medium.com/age-of-awareness/alan-watts-on-the-5-most-important-lessons-of-the-21st-century-6d1734aa6cf*

James, W. (1917). *The Varieties of religious experience.* NY: Longmans, Green and Co.

Jnana, Y.P. (2018) *Dwelling as a lamp unto oneself.* https://www.wayofbodhi.org/attadipa-sutta-dwelling-as-a-lamp-unto-oneself/

Kierkegaard, S. (1843). *Of Fear and trembling.* London: Penguin Classics.

Lao Tzu. (n.d.). *Tao te ching.* Downloaded December 28, 2020 from http://classics.mit.edu/Lao/taote.1.1.html.

Mirus, J. (2010) *Vatican II on non-Christian religions.* https://www.catholicculture.org/commentary/vatican-ii-on-non-christian-religions/

Most, W. (2020) *The Father William Most collection.* https://www.catholicculture.org/culture/library/most/getwork.cfm?worknum=75

Pascal, B. (2007). *Thoughts, letters and minor works.* NY: Cosimo Classics.

Phillips, U. (2011). *The Preacher and the slave* on *Making speech free CD.* Oakland, CA: PM Press

Rumi. *Mystical Poems of Rumi.* (2009) Chicago: University of Chicago Press.

Sagiv, G. (2017) *Hasidism: A New history.* Princeton, NJ: Princeton University Press.

Sartre, J.P. (1989) *No Exit and three other plays.* NY: Alfred A Knopf, Inc.

Thera, S. (1994) *Kalama Sutta: The Buddha's charter of free inquiry.* https://www.accesstoinsight.org/lib/authors/soma/wheel008.html

Steve. (2007, December 23). *Alan Watts revealed and reconsidered. Naked reflections.* Downloaded from http://nagarjuna1953.blogspot.com/2007/09/alan-watts-revealed-and-reconsidered.html

Tennyson, Alfred Lord. *In Memoriam A.H.H.*D https://www.poetryfoundation.org/poems/45336/in-memoriam-a-h-h-obiit-mdcccxxxiii-27.

Voltaire (1759). *Candide.* (https://www.gutenberg.org/files/19942/19942-h/19942-h.htm)

Watts, Alan. (2013). *The joyous cosmology.* Novato, CA: New World Library.

Author's Biography

A teacher and administrator in public and private schools for close to 40 years, Arthur Yavelberg's career has been dedicated to making complicated concepts and issues accessible to people of all ages and backgrounds. While most of his students were middle schoolers, he has also been involved in teaching World History, American History, and Comparative Religion in high schools and adult education programs around the country. Where many academicians seem to delight in abstruse jargon that confuses more than it explains, his goal has always been to present information in a manner that does not intimidate, but instead helps the student understand and draw independent conclusions.

Besides his professional career in education, Arthur also had the opportunity to live and teach in Singapore for two years. A microcosm of all Asia--with temples, churches, synagogues, and mosques mere blocks from one another--Singapore is a wonderful place to delve into many different religious traditions. Furthermore, once in Singapore, it is easy to travel to China, Japan, Cambodia and Thailand to experience firsthand how these diverse teachings manifest in a variety of cultural settings. To be able to discuss the precepts with so many devotees--to actually participate in the rituals and celebrations--was an experience that, speaking frankly, seemed difficult to dismiss as just arbitrary happenstance.

Now retired, Arthur has been involved with Contemplative Meditation groups and Buddhist sangha, and is actively involved in exploring such topics in social media. Again, these opportunities have helped deepen his spiritual awareness and encouraged him to share what he has learned with others.

CPSIA information can be obtained
at www.ICGtesting.com
Printed in the USA
BVHW041213210321
603126BV00021B/1679